Core Instructional Routines

Go-To Structures for the 6–12 Classroom

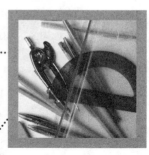

Andrea Honigsfeld and Judy Dodge

HEINEMANN
Portsmouth, NH

Heinemann
361 Hanover Street
Portsmouth, NH 03801–3912
www.heinemann.com

Offices and agents throughout the world

The authors and publisher wish to thank those who have generously given permission to reprint borrowed material:

Autobiographical poem adapted from Bloom, S. J., & Smith, J. M. (1999). Multicultural "autobio" poem. *Electronic Magazine of Multicultural Education*, 1(2), available from http://jonah.eastern.edu/emme/1999spring/bloom.html. Reprinted with permission.

"In How Many Ways Am I Smart?" adapted from *Differentiation in Action* by Judith Dodge. Copyright © 2005 by Judith Dodge. Published by Scholastic Inc. Reprinted with permission from the publisher.

Figure 2.1: From *How the Brain Learns* by David A. Sousa. Copyright © 2011 by David A. Sousa. Published by Corwin Press, a SAGE Company. Reprinted with permission from the publisher via the Copyright Clearance Center.

Figures 3.5 and 3.6: Adapted from *25 Quick Formative Assessments for a Differentiated Classroom* by Judith Dodge. Copyright © 2009 by Judith Dodge. Published by Scholastic Inc. Reprinted with permission from the publisher.

Library of Congress Cataloging-in-Publication Data
Honigsfeld, Andrea.
    Core instructional routines : go-to structures for the 6–12 classroom / Andrea Honigsfeld and Judy Dodge.
        pages cm
    Includes bibliographical references and index.
    ISBN 978-0-325-07434-4
    1. Language arts (Secondary).   2. Middle school teaching.   3. High school teaching.   4. Effective teaching.
5. Classroom management.   6. Curriculum planning.   7. Teaching, Secondary.   I. Dodge, Judith, author.   II. Title.
Curr LB1631.H559 2015
    371.102—dc23   2015021756

Editor: Holly Kim Price
Production: Hilary Goff
Cover design: Suzanne Heiser
Interior design: Bernadette Skok
Typesetter: Gina Poirier, Gina Poirier Design
Manufacturing: Steve Bernier

Printed in the United States of America on acid-free paper
19 18 17 16 15 PPC 1 2 3 4 5

Contents

Acknowledgments vii
Introduction ix

Chapter 1 *BEGINNING-OF-YEAR ROUTINES* 1

Overview.. 1

Beginning-of-Year Routines at a Glance 2

What Does the Research Say About Well-Established Routines
  and Expectations? 3

Beginning-of-Year Routines 4

Special Considerations 24

A Final Thought 26

Essential Questions for Individual Reflection, Collegial Circles,
  and Group Discussions 26

Chapter 2 *BEGINNING-, MIDDLE-,*
AND END-OF-CLASS ROUTINES 27

Overview.. 27

Beginning-, Middle-, and End-of-Class Routines at a Glance 28

What Does the Research Say About Designing Lessons? 29

Routines for the Beginning, Middle, and End of Class 30

Special Considerations 55

A Final Thought 57

Essential Questions for Individual Reflection, Collegial Circles,
  and Group Discussions 58

Chapter 3 **BEGINNING-, MIDDLE-,**
                AND END-OF-UNIT ROUTINES   **59**

Overview 59

Beginning-, Middle-, and End-of-Unit Routines at a Glance 60

What Does the Research Say About Designing Instructional Units? 60

Routines for the Beginning, Middle, and End of a Unit 61

Special Considerations 93

A Final Thought 96

Essential Questions for Individual Reflection, Collegial Circles,
     and Group Discussions 96

Chapter 4 **ROUTINES FOR EACH MARKING PERIOD**   **97**

Overview 97

Routines for Each Marking Period at a Glance 98

What Does the Research Say About Authentic, Student-Driven
     Learning Experiences? 98

Routines for Each Marking Period 99

Special Considerations 121

A Final Thought 123

Essential Questions for Individual Reflection, Collegial Circles,
     and Group Discussions 124

Chapter 5 **END-OF-COURSE ROUTINES**   **125**

Overview 125

End-of-Course Routines at a Glance 126

What Does the Research Say About the Role of Review,
     Self-Assessment, Alternative Assessment, and Reflection? 126

End-of-Course Routines 127

Special Considerations 141

A Final Thought 142

Essential Questions for Individual Reflection, Collegial Circles,
     and Group Discussions 142

References 143

Index 153

Acknowledgments

We are indebted to all the teachers who have implemented effective instructional routines in their classes. Thank you for allowing us into your classrooms and for sharing your lessons, your inspiring learning environments, and your original work with students:

Michelle Ackerman, Mary Andrade, Jessica Antonucci, Brittany Baran, Michelle Berger, Lisa Bing, Matt Blackstone, Hilcia Brandt, Stephanie Brown, Alex Corbitt, April D'Water, Vaughan Danvers, Michele Diaz, Maryclaire Dumas, Bruce Farrer, Brooke Feldman, Jennifer Forrester, Josh Garfinkel, Michael Giamarino, Ken Giosi, Edward Grosskreutz, Michelle Gural, Brison Harvey, Lillian Hsiao, Jeff M. Jakob, Emma Kaveney, Sue Kearns, Vanessa Kittilsen, Sarah Krajewski, George Layer, Amanda Lentino, Robert Lindquist, Anne Logan, Nicole A. Long, Dr. Christian Lynch, Lee Mattes, Dr. Carrie McDermott, Laurence Mechanic, Tyler Messman, Gregory Metzger, Kaitlin Meyer, Dana Moccio, Melissa Nankin, Dan Page, Christine Pearsall, Dr. Gay Pollack, Katie Potter, Michelle Rand, Kathryn Rigley, James Schneider, Heather Stumpf, Shelly Sanchez Terrell, Ellen Van Wie, Jenna N. Waybright, Ramona Woods, Mary Ann Zehr.

We are truly appreciative of all the administrators and instructional leaders who supported this project directly or indirectly. Special acknowledgments go to the following:

Dr. Lisa M. Abel-Palmieri (Director of Technology & Innovation, The Ellis School)

Kathie Acker (Principal, Walt Whitman High School, South Huntington)

Steve Bartholomew (School Photographer, South Huntington Schools)

Dr. Jared Bloom (Assistant Superintendent, South Huntington Schools)

Lori Canneti (Assistant Superintendent, Patchogue Medford School District)

Dr. Cheryl Champ (Assistant Superintendent, Sewanhaka Central High School District)

Maureen Corio (Teacher Specialist for Advanced Academics 6–12, Frederick County Public Schools)

Sharon Deland (Director of ESL, LOTE and Bilingual Programs, Patchogue-Medford School District)

Karen Meier (Joint Chair of English and World Languages, Herricks School District)

Steve Muller (Assistant Principal, Walt Whitman High School, South Huntington)

Rich Roder (Principal, Queens United Middle School)

Steve Toto (Principal, Silas Wood Sixth Grade Center, South Huntington).

We would also to acknowledge the assistance that Kerri Dimitrakakis, a very talented graduate research assistant at Molloy College, has given us throughout the entire manuscript preparation process. Many thanks to Denise Hughes, doctoral program assistant at Molloy College, for the exceptional proofreading of this manuscript. A special thank you to Dr. Audrey Cohan, professor at Molloy College, for being a very supportive critical friend throughout this project and many others.

Last but not least, our gratitude goes to the entire Heinemann staff, without whom this secondary extension of our original K–5 book would not have been possible. We are especially grateful to our acquisitions editor, Holly Kim Price, our production editor, Hilary Goff, our copy editor, Cindy Black, and our marketing manager, Eric Chalek. You and your team brought this book to life and helped us share our vision and passion for best practices in secondary education.

Introduction

What Is Changing?

2015. Almost a decade and a half after No Child Left Behind and five years after the introduction of the Common Core State Standards (CCSS), best practices in secondary education continue to be a hot topic. How can we make sure students are college- and career-ready? Other questions that are just as important include the following: Are they also life- and world-ready? Are they prepared for navigating a global society and making a difference when joining a diverse workforce? The challenge educators face in providing such an education is only compounded by the controversy and deep-rooted debate surrounding large-scale, standardized testing (Burris and Aja 2014), corporate influence on public education (Ravitch 2013), teacher evaluations (Popham 2013), and many other policy and reform concerns (Karp 2013/2014).

> *When students are passionate, they are engaged. When students are empowered, they are unstoppable.*
>
> Vicki Davis, *Social Entrepreneurship: 7 Ways to Empower Student Changemakers*

If students are to succeed with literacy, it will require teachers to work together in professional learning communities to talk about their craft, to reflect upon their practice, to discuss student progress, and to continuously improve their instruction (Fisher, Frey, and Uline 2013). Teachers and administrators, coaches and instructional specialists, and in fact the entire instructional staff will need to come together to discuss what effective teaching and learning looks like in the secondary classroom, what is working and what is not, and what teachers can do to improve their own practice.

We believe that it is important for educators who read this book to understand that the routines we suggest emerge from the existing literature on effective classrooms. The most highly regarded research and investigations into effective classrooms are independent of any paradigm that arises from current educational policy. So, whether the CCSS are retained, modified, postponed, or eliminated, there exists a timeless quality to effective use of classroom time. Simply put, good teaching practice is independent of prevailing policy initiatives, and the routines we suggest will be effective no matter which paradigm is in place when you read this book.

What Are Some of the Greatest Challenges in Secondary Education?

The High School Survey of Student Engagement (HSSSE, pronounced "hessee") is a survey conducted every two years to study student engagement: the attitudes, perceptions, and beliefs of high school students about their work (Yazzie-Mintz and McCormick 2012). Designed and promoted by

Indiana University's Center for Evaluation and Education Policy, the principle goal of this ongoing research initiative is to help high schools explore, understand, and strengthen student engagement.

As Kelsey Sheehy (2013) reported, student engagement nosedives as students move from grade school to high school. Researchers in Indiana go beyond standardized test scores and graduation rates to unpack what is going on with the processes, interactions, and relationships that high students encounter daily (Yazzie-Mintz and McCormick 2012). Data aggregated from HSSSE Spring 2009 show that students do not feel the work is relevant or interesting, and they frequently complain of no interaction with the teacher.

We feel strongly that the routines in this book can make learning in secondary classrooms more relevant and interactive. As your students engage more frequently with you and each other, explore topics of their choice, and become *experts* in their own areas of research, boredom will be relieved for both you and your students.

What Is Going on in a SWRLing Classroom?

We believe the secondary classroom is acutely in need of a shift toward active literacy. A class where we all SWRL!—a move that is marked by every student engaging in meaningful interactions with the new material, with teachers and students *speaking, writing, reading, and listening* every day. We have seen this acronym in several blog posts and recognize it as a powerful synthesizing idea. It reminds us not only to balance what we must do each day in the secondary class but to put the student in charge of her or his own learning. Rather than being passive recipients of learning originating from lectures, PowerPoint presentations, and assigned readings, students internalize new information and skills when they are actively engaged in thinking about, processing, reorganizing, and applying the information (Marzano, Pickering, and Heflebower 2011; Ritchhart, Church, and Morrison 2011).

Teacher-2-Teacher

I quickly learned that the best resource I had for teaching mathematics to my students was the students themselves. I begin my lessons with content as well as language goals. We SWRL every day, that is, we speak, write, read, and listen to the language of mathematics. For example, students discuss the key terms identified in the language goals, do close reading on math problems, review quizzes that are vocabulary-rich in pairs or small groups, and write themselves reflective notes on why they got something wrong and how they can correct it. My classes consist of minilessons that I lead and "hands-on" work that is often collaborative and requires concentrated communication.

Robert Lindquist, mathematics teacher

As Jan Burkins and Kim Yaris blogged after the 2013 International Reading Association Conference, "The best readers and writers are the ones who have had the most practice. How much time do your students spend *actually* reading and writing?" They argue for routines to be established for practicing the four language skills—reading, writing, speaking, and listening—as well as for developing academic language proficiency. If, *regularly*, you prompt students to collaborate, ask them to interact with text, require that they write and communicate ideas clearly, precisely, and with supporting evidence, then all of these skills will strengthen over time because of the consistency of the *routines that you have chosen to put in place*.

Why Routines?

Routines are deliberate procedures that a teacher establishes in her classroom to enhance a sense of community and to offer structure to her learners. Douglas Fisher and Nancy Frey (2009) suggest that the routines that we choose for our classroom should be routines that "over time become the habits of a self-directed learner." They become the shared habits of your classroom community. Students come to know that *this is the way we do things around here*. Dawn Latta Kirby and Darren Crovitz (2013) acknowledge the power of routines and rituals by stating that "it's relatively easy to develop routines for what we like to do, but the more difficult tasks require the discipline of routine if they are to occur regularly and reliably" (68). Many others validate our beliefs about the need for routines. For example, Maureen Boyd and Sylvia Smyntek-Gworek (2012) suggest that

> In classroom communities where literacy events are well-defined, regular practices, teachers establish routines that not only provide a structured space with clear expectations and norms but also opportunity for creative application of what is expected. When students feel safe and valued, they willingly engage, lead, and take risks. (6)

Ron Ritchhart, Mark Church, and Karin Morrison (2011) discuss the need for making thinking visible through *routines*, which in turn may be viewed as *tools* (for promoting thinking), as *structures* (to support and scaffold learning), and as *patterns of behavior* (to establish and maintain a context for learning).

So what does it mean to have routines in the secondary class? For starters, students can count on certain structures to take place regularly and can expect them to be part of *business as usual* in this class. For example, your students may learn that upon entering this classroom, they will regularly complete an Entrance Card or a Do-Now. They may also find that lessons are regularly broken into sections that allow them to stop and process new information, create and reflect on new learning, and meaningfully practice new skills. They may understand that if an interesting question comes up in this classroom during discussion, there will be opportunities provided for independent research to discover the answer or to further explore the question. They may look forward to coming to your class because they know they can count on collaborating with a partner or a group because that's a regular part of each lesson here. The culture of your classroom will depend upon the expectations that you set at the beginning of your course and the choices that you make when establishing routines for each lesson, unit, or marking period. The routines we suggest, however, are aligned with twenty-first-century skills and offer ample opportunities for creative collaboration, critical analysis, meaning making, and student engagement and empowerment.

How Can Routines Help When Teaching Large Numbers of Students a Day?

Routines are even more necessary when you have 100–150 students in one day. With so many students requiring your attention, routines provide a consistency that students can count on and help you smooth the transition from period to period.

Getting your students involved in carrying out some of the managerial routines (gathering homework, passing out textbooks, moving desks into desired arrangements and placing them back at the period's end, etc.) will simplify your day. In addition, the more students are responsible for implementing these routines themselves, the more ownership they will take for the learning that occurs in your class. An analysis done in 2013 by the Center on Education Policy at George Washington University in Washington concluded that among four academic mind-sets that contribute to a student's motivation are *ownership of his or her learning* and a *feeling of social relatedness to the school and community*. When routines make students feel like they are an integral part of the class, motivation increases and sets the stage for students to take responsibility for their own learning. When students are expected to participate in the routines and interact with you in a way that is mutually respectful ("This is what we need to do here now. I can do my part."), the classroom becomes a community of learners where you and your students share responsibility for what takes place daily. By getting some of the essential routines out of the way within the first few days of the course and within a few minutes of each class, you will have more time to spend getting to know your learners and engaging them in the important work of the day. Routines and preestablished structures will be especially beneficial ways to support struggling middle school and high school learners.

What Are Research- and Evidence-Based Best Practices?

John Hattie's (2012) seminal work *Visible Learning for Teachers* synthesizes the largest amount of research on education with a special focus on academic achievement in a way that is accessible to practitioners. He identifies six areas of concentration—the student, home, school, curricula, teacher, and teaching strategies—for identifying the factors with the largest impact upon learning in each of them. The complex results of his meta-analysis point to some critical findings, such as the powerful impact teachers have on their students' learning. Based on his findings, he suggests that "what is most important is that teaching is visible to the student, and that the learning is visible to the teacher" (17). His explanation of what visible teaching is includes making sure the teacher activates and directs learning, creates an environment with deliberate goals that are engaging and responsive to students' needs, and "maintains a passionate belief that students can learn" (25).

How does a secondary teacher reconcile the heavy demands of the content curriculum with best practices in secondary pedagogy, while enhancing students' literacy skills in the content area? Here, we argue that teachers should expand their professional skill sets supported by current research. We provide a practical approach to disciplinary literacy instruction that will also increase students' content knowledge. We will support our claims with numerous research-based instructional practices, resources we adapted, created, or found in teachers' classrooms, and through authentic input from teachers around the United States.

How Is the Book Organized?

We organized this book into five chapters. With the exception of the introductory chapter, each chapter focuses on a different set of routines that support literacy development within and across the content areas. Some routines are ideal when introduced at the beginning of your course, whereas others are best saved for celebrating learning at the end of the course. Some routines are to be employed daily or as frequently as meaningfully possible; yet others will be strategically used only once or twice during a unit or marking period. Because we know that students do not develop or enhance their literacy skills in isolation, many of the routines we suggest here will engage multiple literacy skills.

In Chapter 1, we address the challenges of the beginning of the year and make a case for establishing routines at the onset of your course. Most core middle and high school courses run for the entire year, yet many electives or special courses may begin midyear or at different times throughout the year. Some courses last only one semester—sometimes, they are even shorter. From the very beginning of any course, it is critical for all learners to understand expectations and structures that will be put in place to make learning most productive. In this chapter we make the case for setting clear goals, clarifying expectations, and establishing routines at the beginning of each course. We share engaging icebreakers and short getting-to-know-you and goal-setting routines that set the tone for the year.

Chapter 2 is about establishing routines for the beginning, middle, and end of each class period. When your students understand what they will be learning and doing each day, they will take more ownership for their learning. How can you maximize instructional intensity during your class period, be it forty, sixty, ninety minutes, or longer? The well-established routines that we suggest for opening and closing your lessons will help you do just that! They will provide you choices for offering students strategic opportunities for processing new information and practicing new skills. In the beginning of each lesson, you will establish routines that hook the learner, set the stage for learning, activate prior knowledge, and generally prepare and focus student attention. During each lesson, you will help students focus on processing activities that help them to make meaning and construct understanding. We do this by having learners interact and engage with the material and each other. We put in place routines that help students select, collect, and organize information. We provide opportunities for students to speak with each other using both academic and content-specific language to develop new knowledge, new understandings, and new skills. At the end of most lessons, we want students to integrate and internalize their new knowledge so we ask students to reorganize or synthesize what they have learned. Opportunities are provided for students to reflect on the "takeaways" of the lesson.

Chapter 3 broadens the focus to create predictable routines around instructional units that may last about a week or as long as several weeks. For each unit of study, we propose that you help activate, assess, and build students' background knowledge to maximize their learning of new skills and information. In each unit, a set of routines leads to active peer discussions and collaboration, choice opportunities, and developing academic language and literacy skills in your discipline. The routines that you put in place during the first unit should continue throughout most, if not all, of the units, providing habits that students can count on, such as focusing on academic as well as content-specific vocabulary, taking notes, making arguments, participating in debates, and sharing what they have learned through group presentations to the class.

In Chapter 4, we discuss routines that may take place once a marking period or more frequently, if you have a 90-minute or 120-minute block of time. Pressed for time to cover so much content at the secondary level, you might hesitate to go beyond the course curriculum. Yet, for your students to become engaged and excited about your particular discipline, they must be encouraged to become curious, self-directed leaners who wonder about relevant issues and ideas. Whether your school runs a trimester or quarterly schedule, these once-a-marking period routines provide unique opportunities to engage learners in project-based learning experiences and other student-driven explorations. These routines will take instruction deeper, further, and, often, beyond the classroom walls. Encompassing research, current events, field trips, choice projects, mentors, and so on, you will help students develop skills for lifelong learning when you honor their diverse interests in these ways. Focusing on academic as well as content-specific vocabulary, you will provide students with collaborative opportunities for making arguments, participating in debates, and sharing what they have learned in class through group presentations.

In Chapter 5 we recommend end-of-course routines for consolidating and reflecting upon learning. As with most secondary courses, you are likely to have a final exam as the last requirement for course completion. Yet, we believe in giving students other opportunities to bring closure to your class by allowing them to select from a choice of meaningful, engaging routines.

All chapters have a similar internal organization. Each starts with a brief overview of the goals of the chapter, followed by a graphic organizer that gives you a visual representation of the routines. Then, we provide you with research that supports the suggested instructional routines that come next. A Special Consideration section featured at the end of each chapter will offer you recommendations for differentiating instruction for English learners, students with disabilities, and advanced learners. Peppered throughout the text are photographs taken in classrooms we have visited, Teacher-2-Teacher vignettes, Coach's Notes, essential resources (under the heading Check This Out), samples of student work, and charts for classroom use.

An extensive collection of templates is available for easy reference and reproduction. A companion website will provide ready access to these materials in both Word format and as PDFs, allowing you to adapt the templates. To access the online templates, visit **heinemann.com/products /E07434.aspx** and click on the Companion Resources tab.

Why This Book?

In this book, we offer you suggestions for establishing routines that will build consistency, trust, and a sense of safety in your classroom. By showing students what they can expect and count on, you will be establishing a healthy environment for learning. You will find that many of the routines we suggest in this book interweave multiple literacy skills with the demands of the content curriculum. For example, when students are reading, they will be expected to speak and listen to peers as they all make meaning from text. In addition, it is likely that after a close reading, students will write brief summaries that require the appropriate use of academic language. With daily and weekly routines that integrate multiple skills, you can feel confident that you are providing instruction that will build skills for students to be successful and more independent in secondary school and beyond.

Although standards and mandated or prescribed curricula tell us *what* we must do, this book will help you decide *how* to establish the necessary routines to do it. Whereas many of the current publications suggest the skills, habits, and dispositions that students will need upon graduation, this book will offer you dozens of routines that will contextualize the standards and answer the question, "What does this look like in my secondary classroom?" It will explore the research behind the routines, providing you with the understanding of *why* certain routines lead to better learning. It will show you why routines must be part of every teacher's repertoire if we are to help students achieve greater success.

Specific suggestions will be provided for each set of routines; some of the recommendations will be low-prep; others will require more time to create and implement. You probably have used some of the routines that will be presented, but you may find a new way to accommodate a specific group of learners while using routines aligned to your content curriculum.

Contrary to the belief that routines can lead to dull, repetitive, unimaginative, scripted ways of teaching, we believe that the routines we suggest herein will not only lay the framework for predictable structures, instructional consistency, and skill building but will also provide plenty of opportunity for teacher autonomy and creative expression and will nurture the desire to learn in each child. We, along with thousands of teachers with whom we have worked throughout our combined more than sixty years in the field of education, are convinced that routines can contribute to productive as well as joyful learning.

Well begun, half done!

Proverb

Great things are not done by impulse, but by a series of small things brought together.

Vincent van Gogh

Chapter 1

BEGINNING-OF-YEAR ROUTINES

Overview

In this chapter, we

- summarize research support for the beginning-of-year routines we present
- establish routines for starting the school year (or a new course) successfully
- present examples, templates, resources, and classroom vignettes along with recommendations from coaches to support the implementation of beginning-of-year routines
- discuss special considerations for variations in teaching assignments (large number of students, multiple courses or multiple sections of the same course, varied lengths of class periods) as well as technology integration.

Beginning-of-Year Routines at a Glance

ROUTINE 1 - - → **Icebreakers**

First Impression Routines
- Hopes and Fears
- Yarn-to-Yarn

Getting-to-Know-You Routines
- Autobiographical Poems
- Interest Inventories
- Photo Essay or Collage

ROUTINE 2 - - → **Routines for Establishing a Positive Learning Environment**

Community-Building Routines
- Find Someone Who . . .
- Flexible Grouping
- Artifact Round Up

Routines for Collaborative Class Rules and Expectations
- Class Rules and Promises
- Contracts, Course Outlines, Letters to Students or Families

ROUTINE 3 - - → **Igniting Passion for Your Course**

Routines for Previews
- Course Trailer or Teaser
- Scavenger Hunt in the Textbook
- Visual Tour

Routines for Review
- Carousel Brainstorming
- Nurturing Habits of Mind

Goal-Setting Routines: Personal, Literacy, and Academic Goals
- Getting to Know Yourself as a Learner
- Time Capsule/A Letter or Email to Your Future Self

What Does the Research Say About Well-Established Routines and Expectations?

Both novice and experienced teachers know that day 1 (along with the following few days) in the classroom is likely to set the tone for the rest of the course (Wong and Wong 2004; Wormeli 2003). Whether your course is a semester, a year, two years long—or as short as eight weeks or less—the way you start it will have lasting impressions and implications. Research has shown that students need a sense of belonging and self-efficacy (Bandura 1989, 1991) to reach their potential and thrive in school. Albert Bandura (1989) emphasized the role that self-efficacy plays in motivation when he noted that students' "self-efficacy beliefs determine their level of motivation, as reflected in how much effort they will exert in an endeavor and how long they will persevere in the face of obstacles. The stronger the belief in their capabilities, the greater and more persistent are their efforts" (1,176). As applied to the classroom, when students have an "I can do it" attitude, both their effort and achievement is likely to increase. Instilling and nurturing a can-do attitude in students from the onset of the course will pay off in the long run.

Current trends in motivation theory and research also indicate the importance of recognizing a range of different factors including sociocultural and cognitive ones. M. Kay Alderman (2013) noted that motivation cannot be treated as a stand-alone characteristic of education or a by-product of it; instead, teachers must address it as part of content-based instruction as well as students' socialization process. Ben Dalton (2010) recognized the diversity of definitions and theoretical and empirical research approaches to motivation, yet he concluded that "the evidence for motivation's role is remarkably consistent: intrinsically motivated students, students with high expectations of success, and students with mastery goals are all more likely to succeed than students with alternate motivations" (24). In a recent national survey, the Education Week Research Center (2014) found that student engagement and motivation are the most important factors that contribute to student achievement; educators who participated in the survey reported a range of strategies to motivate and engage their students such as establishing clear goals and expectations, using interactive learning tasks and hands-on activities, building personal relationships with students, making the curriculum interesting and relevant to students' lives, and providing choices and authentic learning opportunities that also foster student autonomy.

It has also been widely recognized that the teaching–learning cycle requires clear goals and Learning Targets communicated by the teacher. John Hattie (2012) found that establishing student expectations, and as a result, making learning visible for students, is the highest-ranked influence on student outcomes. Very highly ranked are the following influences as well: teacher credibility (#4), teacher clarity (#9), and student–teacher relationship (#12), all of which need to be established early on in the course.

When students (and their parents or visitors) first enter a school, they often have an immediate sense about the type of place it is. Ronald Williamson and Barbara Blackburn (2009a) note that "while the school's climate reflects the 'feeling or tone' of the school, culture reflects the more complex underlying set of values, beliefs and traditions that are present in a school"

(8). It has been well established that school leadership plays an essential role in creating and sustaining a positive school climate and school culture, and we believe that each teacher contributes to creating such an environment. The climate and culture of your classroom depends largely on the routines you establish early on and the core values you and your students collectively embrace every day.

Teacher-2-Teacher

Although establishing routines may seem boring to many teachers, if done correctly, they can help students feel safe and confident. After establishing your routines, allow students to own them by asking students to work in groups to brainstorm examples of what they should look like on a daily basis. You can even have the students take this a step further by modeling each routine. Once your routines are established and embraced by your students, your creative and literature-rich lessons will proceed without breakdowns in classroom management. Melissa Nankin, William Wirt Middle School, Riverdale, Maryland

Beginning-of-Year Routines

What is the first thing you do when you walk into your class on day 1? How do you introduce yourself and your course? How do you communicate what you believe in, what your expectations are, and what shared values you wish to establish? How do you connect with your students and start the semester off on the right foot? There are many different ways to build a climate of trust, to create a vibrant learning community, to set the tone for beginning a new course, as well as to motivate your students and nurture their desire to learn. Here we suggest a number of routines to accomplish the following within the first days and weeks of your course while also nurturing students' literacy skills from the onset of the year:

1. Break the ice and get to know your students.
2. Establish a positive, engaging learning environment with clear goals and expectations.
3. Ignite your students' passion for your course.

The beginning-of-year routines presented here are aligned to these three overarching goals while also maintaining a balance of addressing students' social-emotional, academic, and literacy needs. As Kerry Griswold Fitch (2013) suggests, "We must first teach our students our expectations and how to be successful in our classrooms before we jump into content. When you have procedures and routines in place, your time with students is maximized—and time is a sought-after commodity, whether you come from an affluent district or one battling budget cuts" (paragraph 1). On the other hand, Rick Wormelli (2003) warns against immersing students in an endless stream of warm-ups and getting-to-know-you activities, only to be interrupted with forms to fill out and contracts to sign all day long at the beginning of the school year. Instead, he suggests striking a balance between establishing rapport with the students, teaching them the protocols they need to follow, and diving into the content of your course. He cautions not to miss the window of opportunity for learning "with neurons firing on all thrusters. It's probably the most significant time of the year to hardwire students' minds to embrace our subjects; we don't want to lose it" (19).

Some beginning-of-year routines we present have many variations, some might not apply to your course, yet others will not readily appeal to you. As with all the routines in this book, we encourage you to select the ones that seem most fitting, most convincing, and most promising, or find a way to adapt them to match your own unique approach to starting your course in the best possible way.

ROUTINE 1 Icebreakers

What is a good way to put the students (and you) at ease at the beginning of a new course? Icebreakers may be quick and easy to implement or more elaborate, carefully structured games you play to lower students' anxiety. The hectic nature of the first day of school or the stress of transitioning from elementary to middle school, from middle to high school, or merely from one grade to the next may call for a moment to relax. In addition to games and activities that do not directly relate to the course content, a motivational video produced by students who have recently finished your course (see Chapter 5 for a description of this end-of-year routine) will send a reassuring or inspiring message from prior students to those who are about to start it.

FIRST IMPRESSION ROUTINES

First impressions count. Making sure students feel they matter also counts. The very first activities you introduce to your class may be some First Impression games or other, highly engaging, yet not very stressful opportunities for students to acclimate to your class.

Hopes and Fears

This routine asks students to share their hopes and fears regarding the upcoming school year or, more specifically, your course. Each student receives an index card. In response to a question about the course (specifically about course content or more generically about the learning that will take pace that year), they anonymously jot down their hopes on one side and fears on the other side of the card. For example: What are your hopes and fears about reading Shakespeare? What are your hopes and fears regarding learning French? What are your hopes and fears for the upcoming academic year? Collect the cards, skim through them, and read aloud a few of the fears first. Notice if several students have voiced similar fears and comment on the ones that need immediate reassurance. Next, read aloud several more hopes than you read fears and validate your students' ideas. If needed, offer some clarifications if some of the hopes are not aligned to the course goals. Because it is an excellent informal needs assessment tool, make sure you carefully read all the cards after class and note patterns of fears and hopes that could be revisited or kept in mind for future class sessions.

Yarn-to-Yarn (Also Called String a Conversation Together)

If your class seems reserved, perhaps because students are coming from different feeder schools, it might be beneficial to get them out of their seats and let them talk to each other using a gamelike routine. Prior to class, get a big ball of yarn and cut it into matching pieces of different lengths. You should have two pieces of yarn in each length and one piece of yarn per student in your class. For example, if you have thirty students, you will have cut the ball of yarn into fifteen pairs of equal pieces, ranging from two to fifteen inches or so. Greet students at the door and give each student one piece of yarn. Once they settle down, have everyone find the classmate who holds the matching piece of yarn. When they find their match, students introduce themselves and share some information. A list of prompts can help students extend the basic introductions into a more extended, less awkward conversation. You can bring closure to this activity by inviting students to introduce their partners to the class.

After a First Impressions game, you might choose to continue with one or more getting-to-know-you routines. Despite the large number of students you as a secondary teacher will work with, and regardless of the grade level or content area you teach, one early priority is to establish rapport with your students. Although the First Impressions games and activities already offer a glimpse into students' thoughts and feelings, it must be evident to them that you want to find out who they are and care about every one of them beyond test scores and grades.

GETTING-TO-KNOW-YOU ROUTINES

Although your students will recognize you as a content expert, turning your attention to the students' background defines you right away as the teacher of your students, not merely as the teacher of your subject matter. Find out what their interests and special skills are, what background knowledge and abilities as well as unique needs they bring to your class through some getting-to-know-you routines. Doing this as early in the year or semester as possible contributes to building a sense of belonging in your class and allows for capitalizing on students' talents, knowledge, and skills, socializing them into the school and class culture, and motivating them throughout the year. In a study about adolescents' sense of belonging, Beverly Faircloth (2009) found that "allowing students to engage in learning in ways that are attentive to students' developing sense of their own identity may offer a powerful avenue to establish motivating connections to school" (324). Students need a safe space to affirm their sense of self, to tell their stories, and to connect new learning to their own values, perspectives, interests, and priorities. The routines we suggest here also engage students in different modalities such as speaking, writing, reading, and listening, thus also establishing the expectations for a SWRL-ing classroom (see Chapter 2 for more on that).

Autobiographical Poems

Starting with poetry writing not only introduces literacy into your class early on but also encourages students to express themselves and share about their lives. Autobiographical poems allow students to introduce themselves and connect with you and each other through a creative format. Before they receive one of the templates, students can be asked to reflect upon their own identity and share feelings about their lives and cultural experiences through poems. On the other hand, you might decide that any of these templates are too limiting and have students write in their own preferred format instead. The formats we present here offer structure and a scaffold for students who need it; however, one or more of these can also be used as merely suggested or optional outlines.

Take 1. I am . . .

Start each line with the simple phrase "I am . . ." and invite your students to think of defining themselves through as many lenses as possible: favorite locations, family relationships and friendships, in- and out-of-school experiences, actions, sports, hobbies, foods, and so on. (See www.edchange.org/multicultural/activities/poetry.html for more.)

Take 2. I used to be . . . but now . . .

In a more sophisticated version, offer the option to your students to contrast past experiences and aspects of their identity with more current ones.

Take 3. All about me cinquain

Provide your class with a classic format such as the cinquain, which is a five-line poem that requires a noun for the first line, two adjectives for the second, three verbs for the third, an expression of feeling for the fourth, and in the last line a noun that means the same as the first one. In an adapted version, the first noun should the person's first name and the last noun should be the person's last name. Make the cinquain template available on the board or chart paper to visually scaffold the task for your students:

$$\text{_____}$$
$$\text{_____} , \text{_____}$$
$$\text{_____} , \text{_____} , \text{_____}$$
$$\text{_____} .$$
$$\text{_____}$$

Take 4. Line-by-line scaffolds for an autobiographical poem

Provide a more detailed framework, such as a line-by-line scaffolded outline with specific guidance on the information students are asked to include in their poems.

> Line 1: Your name
> Line 2: *Two adjectives* joined by *and* to describe you
> Line 3: A *verb* and an *adverb* to describe something you like to do
> Line 4: Start with *like* or *as* followed by a comparison
> Line 5: Start with *if only* followed by a wish

Or Line 1: First name
> Line 2: Four descriptive traits
> Line 3: Born in . . .
> Line 4: Who feels . . .

Line 5: Who needs . . .
Line 6: Who gives . . .
Line 7: Who fears . . .
Line 8: Who would like to see . . .
Line 9: Resident of (name of city) . . .
Line 10: Last name
Adapted from Bloom and Smith (1999)

A variation on the autobiographical poem is asking students to write a poem about their names. See Figure 1.1 for a ninth grader's poem on the meaning of his name using some sentence starters that offered scaffolding and guidance.

Figure 1.1 My Name

My name belongs to me.
It means brave, happy, and smart.
It means courageous, funny, and upset.
It is like a cloud wafting through the sky.
It is the color of a million colors all intertwined to make one.
My name is a boat floating through a calm ocean.
My name feels similar to a piece of tasty dark chocolate melting on my tongue.
To me, my name sounds like wind chimes when a breeze passes by.
My name feels like a soft, cozy blanket during a long cold night.
It looks like a bolt of electricity.
If I could have a different name, it would be no different than this one.
It wants to break out of its shell.
In one word, my name is calming.
But it is my name,
And my name is Benjamin.

Interest Inventories

One way to find out what students are interested in outside your class is to have them complete an interest inventory. It might include questions related to both your subject matter and to generic background information about each person. Students' out-of-school, authentic experiences, background knowledge about topics that may or may not be related to the course content, and hobbies and passion for pursuing a nonacademic goal will inform you about the student as a whole person. The interest inventory results may be used in multiple ways:

- **to connect with students on a personal level**
- **to understand unique situations or special challenges students face (such as anything they may reveal about their family lives)**

- to find out about students' special interest and talents that may fall outside of the typical classroom conversation and your content area
- to tailor choice homework or research assignments to students' interests
- to design a "hook" activity to motivate students based on the information given in the inventory
- to discuss short-term and long-term goals, including career choices, with students.

Variations on the interest inventory may include questions and prompts that are more specific to your subject matter. A reading interest inventory asks students about their reading habits: what their favorite authors and recently finished books are, whether or not they visit the local library or do more reading online, and what their preferences are for topics and genres outside school. An interest inventory in any other content areas may ask students about favorite topics covered in previous years, memorable lessons, unique learning experiences, or out-of-school connections. See Figure 1.2 for an interest inventory that you can adapt or expand upon as you see it fitting your needs.

Figure 1.2 Sample Interest Inventory

1. What kind of books do you like to read? What do you learn from them?
   _____

2. What types of TV programs do you prefer? Why?
   _____

3. What is your favorite activity or subject at school? Least favorite? Why?
   _____

4. What is your first choice about what to do when you have free time at home?
   _____

5. What kinds of things have you collected? What do you do with the things you collect?
   _____

6. If you could talk to any person currently living or from history, who would it be? Why? Think of three questions you would ask the person.
   _____
   _____
   _____

7. What are your hobbies? How do they enrich you?
   _____

8. What career(s) do you think might be suitable for you when you are an adult?
   _____

9. What is one more thing that you would like me to know about you?
   _____

Photo Essay or Collage

When technology tools are readily available—such as PCs, laptops, iPads, or tablets—you can have your students create a photo essay or collage about themselves by inviting them to select and arrange images that best depict their lives and identities. Although this task not only taps into and nurtures their visual literacy and information literacy, it allows for an alternate modality for self-expression. Students can share their photo essays and collages either on a class website or in pairs or small groups in class.

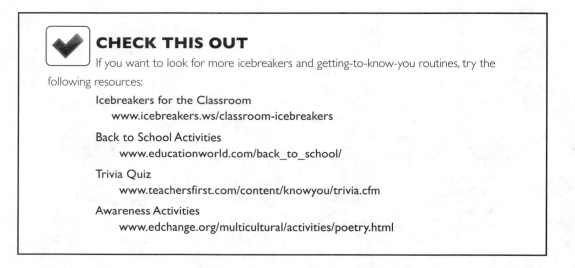

CHECK THIS OUT

If you want to look for more icebreakers and getting-to-know-you routines, try the following resources:

Icebreakers for the Classroom
        www.icebreakers.ws/classroom-icebreakers

Back to School Activities
        www.educationworld.com/back_to_school/

Trivia Quiz
        www.teachersfirst.com/content/knowyou/trivia.cfm

Awareness Activities
        www.edchange.org/multicultural/activities/poetry.html

ROUTINE 2
Routines for Establishing a Positive Learning Environment

Although recognizing each individual who makes up a class is critical, the goal is to turn these individuals into a vibrant learning community through some community-building routines. Most secondary courses begin with establishing class rules and defining expectations. A collaborative approach to creating these goals will ensure student ownership and a higher level of commitment to adhering to these expectations. Finally, before the course begins, you may choose to "take your class to the movies and offer a preview." You might put together a brief video of former students at work in your classroom or images of your content captured from video clips or digital photos. It may not be as loud and exciting as a much-anticipated preview in the movie theater; nonetheless, early access to the curriculum will give students the highlights and evoke excitement about their upcoming course.

COMMUNITY-BUILDING ROUTINES

Community-building routines have long-lasting impact. Although there are many games and activities you can choose from, the ones we suggest here accomplish multiple goals: initiating the process of creating positive interdependence, establishing norms for collaboration, and nurturing a culture of trust in your class.

Find Someone Who . . . (Also Called People Search)

Through this classic activity, students mix and mingle while talking to and finding out interesting details about each other. Start by creating a list of look-fors that include items that are generic and help students learn more about each other as well as items that more or less connect to your own course content. For example, find someone:

who was born in another country

who owns an unusual pet

who has visited New York City

who has more than two siblings

who has been to an art museum in the past two months

who prefers Macs to PCs

who is a _____ (add local sports team's name) fan

who reads and writes in a language other than English

who read the same novel from the summer reading list as you

who has an allergy

who competes on a school sports team

who plays a musical instrument

who watches _____ (add popular teen TV show's name)

who has read the novel *The Hunger Games* by Suzanne Collins (2010).

In an alternative version of this activity, a blank template can be handed out to the students so they could generate the items that they would like to use.

Flexible Grouping

Even if the desks in your classroom are arranged in a more traditional configuration, varied and flexible grouping routines are needed to ensure student-to-student interaction. All learners—students with exceptionalities as well as English language learners—benefit from multiple meaningful opportunities to engage in discussions on the course topic. Don't wait beyond the first week to start setting up routines for group work. Students need to see that sometimes they will be working in pairs, sometimes with three or four other students, and at other times in larger groups or teams. It is critical for all students to understand and have ownership of the grouping routines. Engage in interactive modeling of how students get into the various configurations, how they stay focused on the task, how they report about their accomplishments or bring closure to the task through reflection and evaluation, and how they transition back into a large-group setting. See Figures 1.3 and 1.4 for anchor charts created in secondary classrooms within the first week of the course.

Figure 1.3 Effective and Ineffective Groups

What Effective Groups Do

Look Like
- People <u>LISTENING</u> to each other.
- On task
- Sharing/writing ideas

Feel Like
- Excited/passionate
- Respected

What Ineffective Groups Do

Look Like
- Wandering/off task
- Inattentive/not awake
- Talking is off topic
- Doing non-school things

Feel Like
- Disappointment
- Disrespected
- Frustrating/Aggravating

Figure 1.4 Group Roles

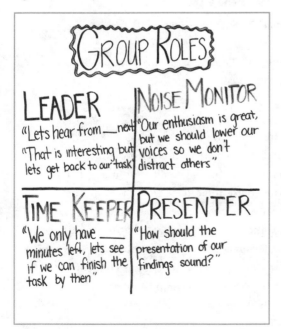

GROUP ROLES

LEADER
"Lets hear from ___ next"

"That is interesting but lets get back to our task"

NOISE MONITOR
"Our enthusiasm is great, but we should lower our voices so we don't distract others"

TIME KEEPER
"We only have ___ minutes left, lets see if we can finish the task by then"

PRESENTER
"How should the presentation of our findings sound?"

Artifact Round Up (Adapted from "My Life in a Bag" [Caruso 1999])

Before the second class, ask students to collect five objects that represent their identity and place them in a bag. Invite students to be thoughtful about these five objects, and ask them to consider multiple dimensions about who they are in and outside of school. When they return to class, form random pairs. Have students exchange bags with their partner and examine each other's objects. Without asking any clarifying questions first, tell students to make assumptions and practice inferring about each other's lives. Have them each assert their beliefs to their partner. Any misconceptions may be corrected after the initial description is over.

ROUTINES FOR COLLABORATIVE CLASS RULES AND EXPECTATIONS

Class rules must be clear and easy to follow, so it is best if students have a substantial role in generating them. By owning the rules and having clarity about shared expectations, students develop a sense of belonging in your class. Pernille Ripp (2014) suggests that "having the students discuss what they expect out of the year and then have them discuss what that means for their learning environment. Students know how to do school. . . . Acknowledge the expertise they bring as veteran 'school' children" (57).

Pernille Ripp's wisdom about giving the classroom back to her students is equally applicable to the middle school and high school contexts.

Class Rules and Promises

Most teachers agree that establishing class rules early on will help students view them as the norm by which to live and work in the classroom. It is important to carve out time in the first few days for this important routine. Although establishing rules or codes of conduct for classroom participation are common, secondary teachers often simply state the rules they want students to follow. We invite you to consider a more student-centered way of establishing a productive learning environment. Imagine a class in which both the teacher and class members make promises about their respective roles and responsibilities. See Figure 1.5 for sample anchor charts with promises.

Figure 1.5 Anchor Charts with Promises

We Promise...
Students
- To be respectful of one another
- To listen carefully to others' comments and questions
- To come to class prepared
- To complete assignments
- To participate in a way that makes this class a place I look forward to coming to

I Promise...
Teacher
- To be fair (But: Fair is not equal; Fair is getting what you need.)
- To make this classroom a safe place to ask questions and make mistakes
- To help you learn, if you don't know something YET.
- To be respectful of you.
- To plan lessons and activities that make this a class you want to come to.

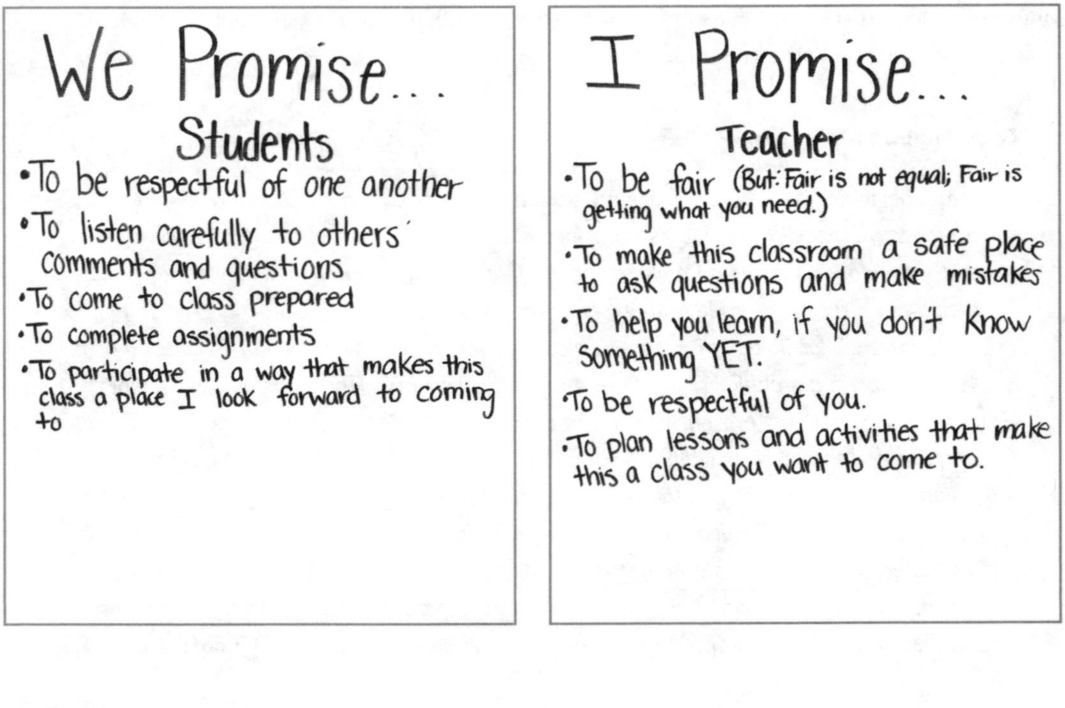

Teacher-2-Teacher

I create a class matrix with my students early in the year. Their input is very important. Professionalism and peer respect is a major focus; this is established in the beginning of the year. Students are expected to contribute regularly in small- and large-group settings and expected to be heard when speaking to others in the class. Students raise their hands but are expected to be ready to participate if called on. Students are professional as they listen to one another, and if a peer is stuck, they are ready to be phoned for help. (See Figure 1.6 for the class matrix my class and I created collaboratively.)

Carrie McDermott, high school English as a second language teacher

Figure 1.6 Class Matrix Found in Carrie McDermott's High School Science/English as a Second Language Class

Classroom Expectations	Entering or Exiting	Small-Group Work	Whole-Group Instruction	Individual/Seat Work	Transitions in and out of the Classroom
Be Responsible	Be in your seat when the bell rings, begin warm-up promptly, have your materials, organize your belongings, sharpen pencil upon arrival, be ready to work.	Share the workload, do your part, begin work promptly, pay attention, ask questions if you are not sure, keep other group members on track.	Begin assignment promptly, pay attention to the speaker, raise your hand, follow directions.	Raise your hand to be helped, do your best work, begin warm-up promptly, stay on task.	Bring necessary materials with you, move quietly and quickly, follow the teacher's signals.
Be Respectful	Enter or exit quietly, greet your teacher and classmates, be polite to your classmates, follow the teacher's directions, hold the door, ask for permission.	Do your part, listen to others, don't interrupt, use the materials appropriately, take turns, stay on task.	Follow directions, listen and respond appropriately, make eye contact with the speaker, participate actively, sit appropriately.	Raise your hand to be helped, do your best work, work quietly and remain seated, stay on task.	Help someone with their belongings, say "Excuse me," be polite, organize your belongings.

continues

Figure 1.6 *Continued*

Classroom Expectations	Entering or Exiting	Small-Group Work	Whole-Group Instruction	Individual/ Seat Work	Transitions in and out of the Classroom
Be Safe	Be in your seat when the bell rings, have your belongings in the correct area, enter calmly, know what to do in case of emergency.	Keep your hands and feet to yourself, organize your group's materials, work quietly, listen to the teacher's directions, keep your chair and feet on the floor.	Organize your belongings, follow teacher's directions, keep your chair and feet on the floor.	Organize your belongings, keep your chair and feet on the floor, follow the teacher's signal.	Follow the teacher's directions, walk, push in your chair, be quiet, be aware of your surroundings, carry materials/ equipment carefully.

Contracts, Course Outlines, Letters to Students or Families

A frequently used beginning-of-year document is a formal one- or two-page course contract, course outline, or letter addressed to either the students or the students and their families. Although these documents may vary greatly in format and length, they typically include some similar sections that provide the students with all the essential information related to the course.

Heading: Name of the teacher, course, year, and any other pertinent details are listed.

Course Description with Goals and Expectations: A brief paragraph covers the content of the course.

Textbooks, Materials, and Supplies: The required and recommended readings as well as necessary classroom supplies are identified.

Required Assignments: A brief description of the types of assignments to be expected in and out of class is provided.

Classroom Participation and Absences: The norm for classroom work and how absences will be handled is established.

Grading System or Grading Policy: What constitutes the final grade, what percentage of the grade will be associated with each component, and if and how students may earn extra credits are indicated.

Homework Policy: Typical out-of-school assignments are described.

Extra Help: Days of the week and times of day when students may receive extra support are noted.

Contact Information: Class website and teacher's email and phone number are provided.

Signatures Lines: Teacher, student, and frequently parents as well sign the contract.

Igniting Passion for Your Course

The beginning of the school year or a new course signifies a fresh start for your students: coming to class with anticipation and some expectations and understandings but also with some apprehension about meeting a new teacher, new classmates, new requirements. One way to move beyond the (much needed) routines presented earlier is to focus on the actual subject matter and the disciplinary literacy that sustains it.

ROUTINES FOR PREVIEWS

There are many ways to offer a glimpse into the content of your course. Your students are probably familiar with and seek out previews of movies or video games. The goal of previewing your course is to get students excited about something new they are going to learn in the coming year.

Course Trailer or Teaser

Although your students know how trailers and teasers get them excited about a much anticipated new film or game, a course trailer or teaser would be quite unique for them to see. Although most commercials are fifteen to thirty seconds long, a course trailer is likely to be somewhat longer and not as fast-paced. A two-minute-long, teacher- or student-made video clip or photo montage will capitalize on student familiarity with an effective presentation format while also offering some highlights of the course content, the typical learning activities to be engaged in, and the forthcoming projects or outcomes.

Scavenger Hunt in the Textbook

In addition to, or in place of a text tour, you might choose to make the first encounter with your course textbook a gamelike activity. Have students search for some key information, pictures, images, titles, as well as text features that are unique to your text (glossaries, end-of-chapter questions, sidebar, or end-of-chapter summaries) in the text while leafing through hundreds of pages; they will become less overwhelmed with the volume and more focused on the treasures they can find inside the book. See Figure 1.7 for sample questions crafted for a seventh-grade social studies book.

Consider revisiting the scavenger hunt routine once a marking period or once in each unit to allow more in-depth previewing of chapters if needed.

Visual Tour

In addition to working with the textbook, you might choose a different visual tool or format to accomplish the task of previewing course content. You may choose to offer a visual tour of the content through a (partially completed) illustrated time line in a history class, noting select dates and key historical figures and places but leaving out some others to peak students' interest. A photomontage can show important authors, places of significance, book covers, and other intriguing images for an American literature course. Utilizing their visual literacy skills and activating their prior knowledge, students practice drawing inferences and making connections between and among previous

Figure 1.7 Sample Scavenger Hunt Prompts

1. What is the name of the textbook?
2. How many chapters are there in your book?
3. What is the title of Chapter 6?
4. What Internet sources are referenced at the end of Chapter 14?
5. According to the preface of the book, what is the purpose of the Chapter Summary?
6. What is the definition of the first word in the glossary?
7. What are the key vocabulary terms in Chapter 8?
8. Turn to page 534. What is the name of the organization the first paragraph talks about?
9. How many maps are in Chapter 4?
10. Turn to page 400. What is the first discussion question?
11. What is the title of the table on page 317?
12. Who is pictured in the cartoon on page 531?
13. Who is the author of the letter on page 213 and to whom was it written?
14. Turn to page 454. What does the bar graph present? Where in the text is the same information discussed?
15. According to the book's index, on what pages will you find information on _____?

literacy experiences and the photos in the montage. A science or technology course may also utilize a version of a visual tour by including real objects. Students examine objects that will represent significance in the forthcoming course and make predictions about the uses of the objects and their role in the course content.

Teacher-2-Teacher

One way I get my students interested in world history is to use props they can see and touch. For example, I introduce the study of Japan in the Middle Ages by serving tea. We then read a text about goods and ideas that traveled from China to Japan during that time period. Other than tea, goods and ideas that Japan adopted from China include bronze technology, Buddhism, and kilns to make pottery. In addition, I use props to teach about the Columbian Exchange, the introduction of goods from the Americas to Europe and from Europe to the Americas after Christopher Columbus landed in the New World. I purchase various goods from the grocery store, such as chocolate, rice, corn, and potatoes, and have students place them on a floor map of the world to show whether the item was introduced to the Americas or to Europe with the Columbian Exchange.

Mary Ann Zehr, history/English as a second language teacher at
Woodrow Wilson High School, District of Columbia

ROUTINES FOR REVIEW

Many middle school and high school courses are designed to be sequential and require students to recall foundational skills and knowledge established in previous grades. Even if your course does not directly build on a previous one, prior learning experiences and sound learning habits are important. Activating students' prior knowledge serves as a powerful link to new learning. According to Robert Marzano (2004), building background knowledge "should be at the top of any list of interventions intended to enhance student achievement" (4). Reviewing some essential information or fundamental skills at the onset of the course as well as at the beginning of each unit will contribute to students' readiness for new material.

Carousel Brainstorming

Although Carousel Brainstorming is ideal for an end-of-unit review of essential learning, it is also used by many teachers to find out what students already know about the upcoming course content. In a Carousel Brainstorm, groups of students move from chart paper to chart paper, writing and sketching to reflect their understanding of subtopics designated by the teacher and posted on the charts. In random groups of four to five students maximum, the students discuss together prior knowledge that they may have around each subtopic and take turns writing or creating bulleted lists in the colored marker assigned to their group. Your job is to facilitate the groups and work with students who need scaffolding.

COACH'S NOTES

Keep in mind that one of the greatest benefits of this routine is the dialogue that will take place among your students. Don't expect a quiet classroom at this time, but do provide suggestions for keeping students focused and on task. Agree on a signal to bring the whole class together either for a point of information (an idea that you think will assist students in this routine after the carousel has already begun) or to remind the groups that all ideas are to be valued.

Nurturing Habits of Mind

Unless they have practiced *activating* their background knowledge as a regular routine in their classroom, some of your secondary students are likely to be passive during a new learning experience, preferring to wait and be told how the current lesson connects to other concepts they might know about. Art Costa and Bena Kallick (2000), in their well-known series of books on The Habits of Mind, remind us that certain habits must be practiced over and over so that learners are "more disposed to draw upon the habits when they are faced with uncertain or challenging situations" (Book

Two: *Activating & Engaging Habits of Mind* 2000, xiii). Among these sixteen habits are some that are ideal to foster in any secondary classroom from the onset of the course or academic year:

- applying past knowledge to new situations
- questioning and posing problems
- thinking with empathy
- thinking about thinking (or engaging in metacognition)
- striving for accuracy
- persisting
- thinking interdependently (or working collaboratively with others)
- thinking and communicating with clarity and precision.

In schools where Art Costa and Bena Kallick (2000) have seen success with students activating their own habits of mind, students talk about, reflect upon, and document the habits of mind that they are focusing on in logs and journals. We recommend choosing select habits and cultivating them throughout the year to help your learners become even more self-directed and fully responsible for their own learning.

 CHECK THIS OUT

Costa and Kallick's (2000) Habits of Mind: A Developmental Series, published by the Association for Supervision and Curriculum Development (ASCD), will provide you with great ideas for teaching students to engage and sustain the types of dispositions needed when learners are confronted by challenges or new problems to solve. Without these habits of thought, as John Dewey (1933) called them, students are more likely to just call upon what they already know, rather than ponder new possibilities. The New Generation of Science Standards call for a shift to problem solving in all science activities. Costa and Kallick's habits of mind will evoke the kind of thinking necessary to engage in this type of pursuit.

For more information, see these related websites:

www.instituteforhabitsofmind.com

www.habitsofmind.org

www.artcostacentre.com/index.htm

www.mindfulbydesign.com

GOAL-SETTING ROUTINES: PERSONAL, LITERACY, AND ACADEMIC GOALS

John Hattie (2009, 2012) claims that it makes a visible difference when students set their own expectations for learning and teachers understand and align instruction to them. Further, he suggests that the ultimate goal of education is for students to become their own teachers and to develop independence and self-regulation during the teaching–learning process. For students to be able to achieve that, they must be given the opportunity to reflect both on their learning profiles and learning needs.

Getting to Know Yourself as a Learner

We addressed getting-to-know-you routines earlier as an approach to breaking the ice and establishing a learning community in the classroom. The purpose of the getting-to-know-yourself-as-a-learner routine is quite different. Here we want to make sure that your students understand how to recognize their own strengths, as well as challenges, and that they become self-directed, independent learners during the course of their secondary education.

In How Many Ways Am I Smart?

Instructions to Students: Think about your own preferred way of demonstrating new knowledge. Read through the following checklist and select the ones that indicate your top six to eight choices. This will help me plan the types of activities to offer you during this upcoming course.

Verbal–Linguistic
- Write a book, poem, myth, or news article about . . .
- Design a checklist for . . .
- Research a topic and take detailed notes . . .
- Write a newsletter . . .
- Create a set of news headlines . . .
- Create concise yet meaningful tweets about . . . .

Logical–Mathematical
- Conduct a survey, graph your results, and draw conclusions . . .
- Construct a visual time line . . .
- Design and conduct an experiment to prove . . .
- Create a game that reinforces understanding of . . .
- Complete a graphic organizer . . .
- Create a word problem based on . . .

Bodily–Kinesthetic
- Bring hands-on materials to demonstrate . . .
- Make a video recording of . . .
- Create a museum exhibit to show . . .
- Create a play, role-play, or use props . . .
- Gather a treasure chest/artifact box to show . . .
- Create a movement or sequence of movements to explain . . .

---

continues

Intrapersonal

- Keep a diary or learning log about . . .
- Reflect on your own learning process . . .
- Write an advice column . . .
- Record in a progress chart your accomplishments toward a goal . . .
- Create a historical or literary scrapbook (about a character, historical figure, inventor) . . .
- Complete a Venn diagram that compares you and a character or historical figure . . .

Interpersonal

- Evaluate your group's performance . . .
- Present a new show/host a talk show . . .
- Interview several people about . . .
- Lead a group discussion on . . .
- Teach the class about . . .
- Conduct a group or class meeting to discuss . . .
- Write and print series of text messages to your friend explaining how to . . .

Spatial

- Design a greeting card or postcard . . .
- Create a photo journal about . . .
- Create a game that teaches the concept of . . .
- Find examples of fine art, architecture, or sculpture to symbolize the plot of a literary selection/reflect the time period . . .
- Take/use photographs to . . .

Musical

- Interpret a song from a specific time period . . .
- Gather examples of music that reflect the mood of a reading or a historical time period . . .
- Analyze different types of poems for their patterns of rhyme, rhythm, or sound . . .
- Play a piece of music to illustrate . . .
- Make an instrument and use it to demonstrate . . .

Naturalist

- Develop a photo journal about . . .
- Take a virtual field trip via the Internet to . . .
- Create a Pinterest board about . . .
- Gather a collection of artifacts that . . .
- Email keypals in other places to learn . . .
- Use binoculars, microscopes, telescopes, or magnifiers to . . .

Adapted from Dodge, J. 2006. *Differentiation in Action.* New York: Scholastic.

Time Capsule/A Letter or Email to Your Future Self

You might have heard the story of Mr. Bruce Farrer—a retired English teacher from Canada—who collected letters written by his students to their future selves when they were fourteen, and then twenty years later tracked the students down and mailed the letters back to them (Stump 2014). You don't have to wait twenty years. Invite students to reflect on their own goals for the course, the entire school year, or the whole middle school or high school experience. You can prompt them to think of different types of goals. Based on your course content and the class composition, you might guide your students to define generic personal goals, general academic goals, course-specific content goals, and even literacy and language-learning goals. Once they have sketched out these goals, have them write a letter to themselves. Invite them to be as specific as possible on what the goals are and how they envision the goals will be met. What tools and supports do they need? What resources do they already have and what are they hoping to receive from you?

Barbara Blackburn (2014) puts a special spin on the beginning-of-year letter writing by referring to it as a *vision letter*:

> *Ask your students to imagine it is the last day of school. Being in your social studies class, for example, turned out to be your (the students') best year ever. What happened? What made it the best year? What did you do? What did your teacher do? Why was sixth grade social studies the best year ever?* (paragraph 3)

Your students will agree that writing to themselves is easy because they are addressing the letter to someone they know the most. At the same time, it is also highly challenging because it is very personal. Telling students that you will not be reading their letters if they mark it *confidential* and even handing them an envelope in which to place and seal their letters may further contribute to building trust and establishing a soon-to-be thriving, respectful learning community.

Teacher-2-Teacher

My ninth-grade students write a letter to themselves on the first or second day of school, describing their feelings about the upcoming school year: what they're excited about, what they're nervous about, what they hope high school will be like. I collect the pieces, then I store them away and surprise the students on the last day of school with the letters (even if I tell them they'll get them back on the last day of school, they don't usually remember me saying it). Their response when they read the letters? Laughter, mostly loud laughter, and phrases like, "No way!" and "Oh my God!" and "Yikes! I can't believe I wrote like that! Thank you so much for making me a better writer, Mr. Blackstone!" Maybe that last part I made up, but I'm sure at least a few students have said it—or at least thought it—over the years.

Matt Blackstone, English teacher, Great Neck North High School, New York

CHECK THIS OUT

In addition to the ideas presented in this chapter, there are a lot of resources available to help you choose the right way to begin and maintain the year or your course.

Resources on Student Motivation and Engagement

Books

Burgess, D. 2012. *Teach Like a Pirate: Increase Student Engagement, Boost Your Creativity, and Transform Your Life as an Educator.* San Diego, CA: Dave Burgess Consulting.

Jackson, Y. 2011. *The Pedagogy of Confidence: Inspiring High Intellectual Performance in Urban Schools.* New York: Teachers College Press.

Lemov, D. 2010. *Teach Like a Champion: 49 Techniques That Put Students on the Path to College.* San Francisco: Jossey-Bass.

Parsons, J., L. Taylor, and University of Alberta. 2012. *Student Engagement: What Do We Know and What Should We Do?* Edmonton, Canada: University of Alberta.

Stern, M. 2012. *Evaluating and Promoting Positive School Attitude in Adolescents.* New York: Springer.

Websites

Edutopia Links

www.edutopia.org/blogs/tag/student-engagement

www.edutopia.org/student-engagement-resources

Great Schools Partnership: Glossary of Educational Reform

http://edglossary.org/student-engagement/

Special Considerations

Classes are diverse and vary on so many dimensions: Your course content and your student population are obviously the first couple of such dimensions, but also consider the tremendous diversity that exists across secondary classrooms in the United States: class, school, and district size; state and local standards and curricula; geographical location; access to resources; use of instructional materials including technology!

What if you teach over 100 students each day?

Getting to know and personally connect with over one hundred students will be a challenge. Yet, the first few days of the course reverses the roles—you will be doing most of the learning and studying: Your rosters, interest inventories, game cards, poems written by the students, and student submissions can all be color-coded so you can easily connect students to class sections, rosters, or courses you teach.

What if you teach multiple courses each semester?

Most of the beginning-of-year or course routines are crosscutting by nature; they can be used across all grade levels and all content areas. If you have multiple sections of the same course or even if you teach different courses each semester, there is no need to have a separate set of routines for each class. Your students will make them unique. Not all games, routines, and activities we suggest here will be implemented in every class, so you may wish to select which subroutines to save for which class as long as you ensure that you establish rapport with the students, build a positive classroom environment, set clear goals, and engage students in exciting learning about your course content right away.

What if you don't have your own classroom?

Traveling from classroom to classroom and sharing a classroom will present some limitations only regarding the routines that require posting students' work on a bulletin board. If you can negotiate the wall space with other teachers who also use the same room at other times during the day, it is a good idea to carefully select what information (anchor chart about class rules) should be posted, what information can be temporarily made available and then rotated, and what information may be best shared electronically, such as via a class website.

What if your class period is longer than the typical forty- to forty-four-minute class?

A longer class period seems to lend itself to doing more of the beginning-of-year routines presented here; however, a better choice would be to carefully select the few routines that yield the most useful information about your students and best match your own teaching philosophy. "Filling" the entire class time—especially a double period—with introductory routines may become repetitious; instead, plan to introduce some of the most intriguing aspects of your academic content right away and spend more time on engaging students in establishing their personal and academic goals.

What if you want to incorporate technology?

From day one, students will see the extent to which you are ready and willing to use technology. Is there a class website where students can check daily in-class and homework assignments, readings, due dates for projects? Will there be opportunities to use technology tools such as laptops or tablets in the classroom on a regular basis? Establishing an easy-to-access course website will reduce any student anxiety or ambiguity regarding the daily learning tasks and assignments. An extension of a course website is a course blog that houses brief commentaries and extension of class discussions. You might even want to encourage your students to create their own blogs on the topic of your course. Almost any of the routines suggested in this chapter will have a technology-based alternative. For example, Aditi Rao (2012) suggests using twenty-first-century icebreakers by creating tech-savvy versions of commonly known getting-to-know activities. When students write letters to their future selves, you can hand them a piece of paper or even some fancy stationery. Alternately, you can introduce a free website to your students (https://www.futureme.org) and have them write an email that you can preset to be released on a certain date. Your scavenger hunt activity can be enhanced by creating QR codes (http://qrcode.kaywa.com) as long as iPads or other devices with a QR code reader are available. Students find answers to prompts by tracking down information presented behind QR codes.

A Final Thought

Remember that your class is just one of seven, eight, or occasionally even nine that students participate in each day. Most teachers are likely to have similar plans to start the year with routines and protocols, so make sure that the first few days do not become repetitive or uninspiring. If you can, coordinate with fellow teachers the types of routines you will each use. Another suggestion is to align course expectations regarding commonly established policies such as homework submission, lateness, missed classes, use of online tools, and so on for consistency.

Essential Questions for Individual Reflection, Collegial Circles, and Group Discussions

- *How do you achieve a balance between procedural routines and a highly engaging, content-focused introduction to your course?*

- *If you had to prioritize your beginning-of-year routines, which one or ones would you choose to give more attention?*

- *What is the most successful beginning-of-year routine that you have developed, adapted, and refined over the years? To what do you attribute its success?*

- *What advice would you give your fellow teachers on establishing routines early on in the course?*

- *What are the benefits of using beginning-of-year routines? How will they help you? And your students?*

The best thing about being a teacher is that it matters. The hardest thing about being a teacher is that it matters every day.

Todd Whitaker, Twitter post

Ideal teachers are those who use themselves as bridges over which they invite their students to cross, then having facilitated their crossing, joyfully collapse, encouraging them to create bridges of their own.

Nikos Kazantzakis, writer and philosopher

Chapter 2

BEGINNING-, MIDDLE-, AND END-OF-CLASS ROUTINES

Chapter 7

Overview

In this chapter, we

- summarize research support for the routines we present
- establish routines for the beginning, middle, and end of a class
- present examples, templates, resources, and classroom vignettes along with recommendations from coaches to support the implementation of class routines
- discuss special considerations for variations in teaching assignments (large number of students, multiple courses or multiple sections of the same course, varied lengths of class periods, technology integration).

Beginning-, Middle-, and End-of-Class Routines at a Glance

ROUTINE 1 - - ➤ **Beginning-of-Class Routines**

Focusing and Guiding Routines
- Learning Targets

Powerful Questioning Routines
- Blooming Questions
- Partners' Inquiry

ROUTINE 2 - - ➤ **Middle-of-Class Routines**

Processing Routines
- Reflect and Connect!
- Academic Vocabulary
- Turn-and-Talk
- Stop-and-Jot

Flexible Grouping Routines
- Socratic Circles
- ThinkTank

Skill-Building Routines
- Close Reading

Note-Taking Routines
- Scaffolded Notes
- Column Note Taking
- Interactive Notebooks
- Dialectical Journals

ROUTINE 3 - - ➤ **End-of-Class Routines**

Lesson Summary and Reflection Routines
- Exit and Choice Exit Cards
- Academic Journals/Learning Logs

What Does the Research Say About Designing Lessons?

Planning and effectively delivering instruction has been a complex topic in the field of education. Madeleine Hunter's (1984) work developing a seven-step lesson plan structure has dominated classrooms for decades. Her framework includes the following steps: (1) review, (2) objectives, (3) anticipatory sets, (4) direct instruction and modeling, (5) checking for understanding, (6) guided practice, and (7) independent practice. Many variations of this format exist; however, most recently, Fisher and Frey (2014a) have revised and expanded this sequence for the following key components to be included in a lesson plan: identification of the topic/theme unit, purpose, standards addressed, essential questions, and materials/resources.

The body of this lesson plan includes four major steps; this lesson planning involves deciding on what will be explored during (1) focused instruction, (2) guided instruction, (3) productive group work or collaborative learning, and (4) independent practice.

During focused instruction, we make sure the lesson's purpose is clear to students so they can make a direct connection between the lesson topic and prior learning. Guided instruction ensures that students are challenged at their level of readiness and actively participate while they respond in a variety of methods and modalities. During collaborative learning, students engage in hands-on experiences and practice with a new concept, whereas independent learning deepens their understanding of a new concept. The lesson ends with formative assessment measures that help plan for future lessons. The instructional framework for the gradual release of responsibility with its four components has become widely recognized and attributed to Fisher and Frey, but they base their work on the original research of Piaget (1952), Vygotsky (1978), and Pearson and Gallagher (1983), as well as the contributions of Wood, Bruner, and Ross (1976) on scaffolded instruction.

Hattie (2012) established six conclusions regarding achieving excellence in education. His signposts toward excellence included recognizing teachers' roles and responsibilities that have a lasting impact on student learning. One of these signposts clearly stated

> *Teachers and students need to know the learning intentions and the criteria for student success for their lessons, know how well they are attaining these criteria for all students, and know where to go next in light of the gap between students' current knowledge and understanding and success criteria of "Where are you going?", "How are you going?", and "Where to next?" (19)*

Dean and colleagues (2012) also suggested that once the learning objectives are determined for a lesson, they must be made clear to the students. In addition to posting them visibly, teachers must refer back to them throughout the lesson, providing opportunities for students to connect the learning experiences to the objectives as well as to previous lessons. These connections will help students place the new learning in context (Dean et al. 2012; Marzano 2003).

Although universal design for learning (UDL) is primarily considered a curriculum design process (Novak 2014), its principles are helpful for daily lesson planning. (See www.udlcenter.org for more information.) The three primary principles of UDL are to provide multiple means of

1. Representation—the content of the lesson is presented in multiple formats thus ensuring that all students can access it and transfer it to new knowledge:
   a. multiple perceptual modalities (auditory, visual, tactile, kinesthetic) infused in the lesson
   b. language-based, visual, or symbolic presentation of content
   c. variety of opportunities for comprehension.

2. Action and Expression—during the lesson students have options for expressing and demonstrating what they have learned and can do:
   a. physical involvement and movement during the lesson
   b. choice opportunities for responding to the content of the lesson (including use of tools and multimedia)
   c. purposeful use of strategies and resources.

3. Engagement—students are motivated and engaged in the lesson in multiple ways:
   a. authentic and relevant learning experiences
   b. fostering collaboration and communication
   c. encouraging goal setting, self-assessment, and reflection about the learning process.

The routines and structures we suggest are built upon the principles noted by Hattie, Fisher and Frey, Marzano, Novak, and others.

Routines for the Beginning, Middle, and End of Class

In the beginning of each lesson, routines will help you to hook the learner, to set the stage and environment for learning, by focusing your students' attention on the forthcoming lesson and guiding their thinking with powerful questioning routines. By making a commitment to activating and assessing background knowledge during this part of the lesson, your students are more likely to make meaningful connections to the new learning.

During each lesson, processing activities will help students make meaning and construct their own understanding. We do this by having learners interact and engage with the material independently and with each other through flexible grouping configurations. Put in place routines that help students select, collect, and organize information. Provide opportunities for students to speak with each other often. Daily formative assessment practices allow you to check for understanding and helps inform your instructional decisions.

At the *end* of our lessons, we want students to be able to summarize, integrate, and internalize their new knowledge, so we ask them to reorganize what they have learned. Opportunities are provided for students to reflect on the essential outcomes or takeaways from the lesson. These routines help make the learning stick (Heath and Heath 2007) before we move on to a new topic or students move on to another class.

Don't be worried if the beginning, middle, and end of your lesson spans more than one class period. We define a lesson as the smallest unit of instruction with a beginning, middle, and an end, rather than as a class period measured in minutes.

ROUTINE *1* Beginning-of-Class Routines

At the beginning of class, it is important to grab your students' attention. In many classrooms, Learning Targets provide this focus for students. In other classrooms, a Do-Now hooks learners. A motivational opening to a lesson (a photograph, piece of music, thought-provoking questions, or a demonstration of a natural phenomenon) stimulates enthusiasm for the content of the lesson. Guide students to answer your focused questions until you explicitly teach them to formulate their own.

FOCUSING AND GUIDING ROUTINES

When designing lesson plans, consider when students are most attentive during a lesson and when their attention is likely to wane. (Refer to the Figure 2.1 where David Sousa describes student attention during a class period.) During a learning episode, we remember *best* that which comes first, *second best* that which comes last, and *least* that which comes just past the middle. Sousa (2011a) calls these episodes *prime-time-1*, *prime-time-2*, and *down-time*. He suggests that during prime-times-1

Figure 2.1 Retention Varies During a Learning Episode

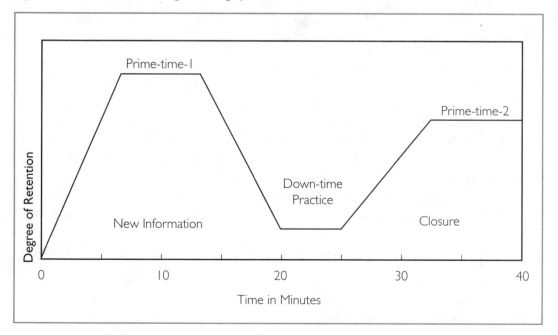

and -2, we teach new information, and during down-time, we have students practice or discuss the new learning, or engage in managerial tasks.

Teachers often give students a Do-Now at the beginning of class and immediately follow up with managerial tasks like checking homework, handing back yesterday's homework or test, taking attendance, and so on. This is an inefficient use of learning time because the time of greatest retention takes place during the first minutes of class. Instead, perform these administrative tasks before you secure student focus with a Do-Now, or handle them during a down-time. Because these first eight to ten minutes are so critical to learning, be mindful of what students are doing.

Learning Targets

Learning Targets give students the language to discuss what they know and what they need to learn. This routine helps students develop independence. It makes students part of the learning process, so the goals for each day are held by the learner, not just the teacher.

Teacher-2-Teacher

As I begin a new lesson with a Learning Target, I think about the Common Core State Standards as well as the language standards for English language learners. I use the acronym SWRL to remind me that I should always plan activities where students speak, write, read, and listen as they actively engage and communicate with each other. I am merely a facilitator and the students are the active participants. At the end of the lesson, students are surprised to see how much they have learned when they reflect on our Learning Target.

Hilcia Brandt, middle school English to Speakers of Other Languages (ESOL) teacher

Connie M. Moss and Susan M. Brookhart (2012) explain how using a *Learning Targets routine* at the beginning and end of each lesson, one that students understand and are required to use throughout the lesson, helps students focus on the intended learning for the day. The Learning Target must be specific, skill-oriented, and measurable, and it should be written in concrete, student-friendly language, beginning with the stem "I can . . ." Keep in mind that the Learning Targets describe the learning outcome, not the activity or the task students engage in. In this way, students can engage in self-assessment and track their own learning.

The following examples are Learning Targets closely aligned to the Common Core State Standards (National Governors Association 2010) that describe the expectations in an eleventh-grade English classroom over the course of several weeks:

Learning Targets
- I can cite strong and thorough textual evidence that supports my inferences and analysis of the text.
- I can determine two or more themes in a text.

- I can analyze the impact of word choice on the meaning or tone of a text.
- I can determine the author's point of view in a text.
- I can synthesize multiple sources on a subject and demonstrate the subject under investigation.
- I can follow a standard format for citation in my work.
- I can use evidence from informational text to support analysis, reflection, and research in my writing.

POWERFUL QUESTIONING ROUTINES

Being able to ask questions of a text on their own indicates students' readiness to read and learn, independent of the teacher. However, most of our secondary students have come to expect that they will only have to answer teacher-produced questions, rather than to think more autonomously. To prepare our students to meet our expectations of generating the academic conversation around a text or topic without teacher facilitation (Danielson 2013), you can begin explicitly teaching question formulation by, first, using the *Blooming Questions routine* and, then, by moving on to the *Partners' Inquiry routine*.

Blooming Questions

Combining levels of Bloom's taxonomy, two at a time, we suggested a *Blooming Questions routine* (Dodge and Honigsfeld 2014) that illustrates for students how different types of questions evoke different levels of thinking. With this routine, we can demonstrate for learners how we move from concrete or basic thinking processes, to more abstract, inferential ways of thinking. See Figure 2.2 for a generic set of Blooming Questions.

Figure 2.2 A Generic Set of Blooming Questions at Three Levels of Thinking

Level A Questions Concrete	Level B Questions Interpretive	Level C Questions Critical and Creative
Can you list ___?	Can you illustrate the conflict?	What if . . . ?
Can you describe ___?	How does ___ compare to ___?	Can you create your own . . . ?
Can you identify ___?	What evidence can you provide for ___?	Would the author of this article agree with the following statement: ___? How do you know?
What are the steps in ___?	Can you describe the motivation of the main character when she ___?	How is ___ still felt today?

continues

Figure 2.2 *continued*

Level A Questions Concrete	Level B Questions Interpretive	Level C Questions Critical and Creative
Can you give some examples of ___?	Can you explain how ___? Can you explain why ___?	Where will the main character be in ten years?
Can you match___ to ___?	What is the point of view of author? How do you know?	Evaluate. Solve for x: $\log_5 x = 2$
What is the length of the hypotenuse of a triangle whose sides measure 36 mm and 42 mm?	How do these documents support President Truman's point of view? How do they contradict his viewpoint?	How is the theme/conflict/ problem in this story like something we experience today in our community?
Can you define ___?	Solve for x. $8x + 7 = -6 + 9x$	What does it mean when someone says, ___?
Can you paraphrase what I just read?	What was the effect on others when ___?	Who else would agree with this leader/character/author? How do you know?
What is rotation? What is revolution?	What does the author believe about ___?	Show multiple ways you could solve this problem.
Simplify the expression $(5s)(-2)=$	Why do you think ___?	How would you argue for ___?

Once students have practiced responding to your questions, they will be ready to engage in an even more powerful questioning routine, one where they are expected to generate their own questions. This one change will offer your students the immeasurable opportunity to become autonomous thinkers and self-directed learners (Rothstein and Santana 2011, 2014).

Partners' Inquiry

When students learn how to generate their own powerful questions, it gives them a purpose for reading or understanding—to find answers to their own questions. They learn to wonder, predict, question, or raise an issue for consideration. "Motivated by their interests, students are more likely to engage in the active construction of knowledge, to make real connections, and to remember what they learn" (Fusco 2012). With the *Partners' Inquiry routine*, students use question starters that apply to the highest levels of Bloom's taxonomy. Pairs of students question the text, concept, belief, or subject presented to them in print, a visual, a video clip, a PowerPoint presentation, a piece of art, a model, a minilecture, or by some other representation. See Figure 2.3 for a set of question starters your students can use until they become more facile at generating their own questions. Notice how involved the students in Figure 2.4 are as they collaborate as partners during class.

Figure 2.3 Question Starters for Partners' Inquiry Routine

Why did . . . ?

Why are . . . ?

How did . . . ?

How did people survive this . . . ?

What caused . . . ?

What led to . . . ?

What is meant by . . . ?

What is the relationship between . . . ?

What principle does this represent?

Why must . . . ?

What's the sequence of steps required?

What evidence can you find to support . . . ?

What would happen if . . . ?

What will the result be . . . ?

Would the result have been different if . . . ?

What will the future be like for . . . ?

What would you predict as the outcome of . . . ?

What could help improve the situation . . . ?

Who/what else comes to mind as you read/look at . . . ?

Who else would agree/disagree with this author's point of view?

Figure 2.4 Middle School Students Engage Completely Using Partner Work

Once you actively engage your learners, you are ready to begin today's lesson. However, keep in mind that questioning routines will continue throughout the lesson. Continue to probe your students and encourage them to ask their own questions. If you do not have time to answer their questions, list them on a question kiosk (a bulletin board, a chart, or an easel). See Figure 2.5 for an example of questions that students might ask over the course of a unit. Your students can use the questions for individual choice homework projects (described in Chapter 3), for independent quarterly research assignments, or for small-group projects (described in Chapter 4).

Figure 2.5 A Question Kiosk Related to an Astronomy Unit

ROUTINE 2 Middle-of-Class Routines

During class, it's important to sustain student interest. One way to ensure engagement is by varying student tasks. Asking students to turn to a preselected partner and briefly discuss what they are learning keeps students more involved with the learning. Using flexible groups with assigned tasks reignites students' attention as they are required to be more responsible for their own learning. Teaching students how to select and organize information on their own instead of simply copying a set of notes keeps students more alert during their academic work.

Students benefit, both in your course and beyond, if they learn to take their own notes. Generating their own notes will give your students agency and a purpose for listening. As they learn and apply new skills of independent note taking, annotating text for analysis of language and meaning, engaging in close reading protocols, and using effective academic vocabulary, your students will grow to be more self-directed learners.

PROCESSING ROUTINES

Students must speak and write about their thinking to make sense of what they are learning. Such meaning-making routines will provide the time necessary for students to process information, reorganize it, understand what it is related to, and to decide how it is relevant to them.

Reflect and Connect!

One way to have students embed their learning and make meaning of new information is to reflect on three important vocabulary terms from the day's lesson. Our *Reflect and Connect! routine*, similar to the Association Triangles routine shared in *Conversations with the Thoughtful Classroom* webinar series (2015), is used to help students make connections and show big-picture understanding. (See Figure 2.6 for an example of a science Reflect and Connect! diagram.) Rather than just memorizing isolated facts, students must consider how information is interrelated.

Figure 2.6 Example of a Reflect and Connect! for a Science Lesson

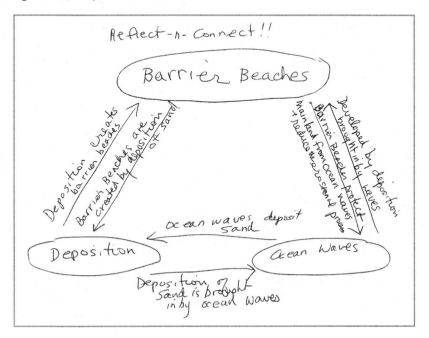

Academic Vocabulary

Teaching vocabulary has been established as a critical part of the K–12 English language arts curriculum and classroom instruction (Marzano 2005). Research has also found that the key features of effective vocabulary instruction "are frequent and varied encounters with target words and robust instructional activities that engage students in deep processing" (Beck, McKeown, and Kucan 2013, 83).

Based on her collaborative work with Isabel Beck and Margaret McKeown, Linda Kucan (2013) promotes a concise, three-step approach that involves a "thoughtful introduction to a set of words, interesting interactions with the words, and assessments of students' knowledge of the words" (364). The vocabulary routine we recommend based on this work consists of the following three steps:

1. Prepare student-friendly explanations for the words that make sense to students. These descriptions should build on age-appropriate dictionary definitions.
2. Engage students in a range of meaningful activities that allow them to use the words in a variety of ways and in a variety of contexts. See the suggestions that follow, as well as student work samples representing varied vocabulary development tasks, many of which involve students' interaction with the words, with the text, and with each other.

3. Use formative assessments to gauge students' understanding as well as productive use of the target words. It's also beneficial to use self-assessment practices such as having students in younger grades put their thumbs up, sideways, or down to show their levels of understanding for key words and having students in older grades use a vocabulary self-assessment rating scale (see Figure 2.7).

Figure 2.7 Vocabulary Self-Assessment Scale

Vocabulary	My Knowledge of Key Words			
	I have never heard of it.	I have heard of it; I think I know what it means.	I know it very well.	I can tell or write a sentence with it.

Researchers have noted the strong connection between vocabulary knowledge and comprehension (Kintsch and Rawson 2005; Perfetti and Stafura 2014). They remind us that vocabulary instruction is critical to understanding. But which words do we choose? Social science teachers might choose discipline-specific words like *democracy*, *monarchy*, *vote*, *government*, *nationalism*, and *capitalism*, and science teachers might choose words like *energy*, *density*, *conduction*, *evaporation*, *isotopes*, *fusion*, *acid*, *base*, and *reactants*.

These *Tier 3 words* (Beck, McKeown, and Kucan 2013) constitute the vocabulary of each content area or discipline. Most students recognize these words after speaking, writing, reading, and listening to them frequently during a class period or over several periods. By SWRL-ing these words (as described in the Teacher-2-Teacher section earlier in this chapter) students come to own them.

However, the words we must also focus on to prepare students to read more complex text are known as *Tier 2 words*. These words are not used as often in class; they tend to be found more in text than in speech; they cross discipline areas and are used in many content areas; they often have multiple meanings. And, up until the Common Core State Standards and new frameworks in the various disciplines became a focal point for discussion about how to improve student comprehension, these words had not been emphasized in most classes. Examples of Tier 2 words include: *trend, rate, shortage, reduction, increase, decrease, shortage, complex, evaluate, analyze, elaborate, usually, descend, dispute, distinct, alternative, advocate, progress, expand, maximum, minimum, abundant, reserved, solitary, suppressed,* and *compassionate*.

Although there are too many Tier 2 words to list in this book, you can easily identify them yourself by reading your past exams, your textbooks, and your previously-used nonfiction article excerpts. Begin to notice the terms that you would normally not make part of a prepared vocabulary list for students, but whose meaning would be needed for students to understand the question or text. See the chart in Figure 2.8 that helps you to reflect by yourself or with a colleague on the Tier 2 and Tier 3 words used in your textbook or previously-given tests.

Academic Vocabulary

Choose a few important passages in your textbook (or informational article) or questions on a previously given test and identify *at least 10 academic vocabulary words and 10 discipline-specific vocabulary words.*

General Academic Vocabulary	Discipline-Specific/Content Area Vocabulary
associated with	economics
diplomatic	river valley
inferred	natural barriers
as a result	capitalism
quota	barter
preserving	child labor
exploit	social system
implement	political corruption
despite	apartheid
assassination	refugees
debilitating	archaeological
scarce	turning points

Once you've identified these academic words, how do you make them familiar to students? How might they internalize these words? In our experience, the answer lies in creating and using an Interactive Academic Word Wall. Here's how it works:

- **Post these words in a place that is visible and easily accessible to your students (on a bulletin board, on a trifold poster, on index cards taped to the side windows, on the inside of a door that you open during each class, etc.). Make sure to choose one or two words each day that you pepper throughout your lesson and make obvious to students (repeating them loudly and pointing to their placement on the word wall). Students will begin to notice their relevance in discussion and look to use the word wall when they are engaged in group communication or individual writing tasks.**
- **Use these academic words while posing questions to students and require that students use them in their responses, as well.**
- **Require students to use one or two of these words appropriately in their writing.**
- **Encourage students to refer to the Interactive Academic Word Wall and to use the words with each other during class to promote discussion. Motivate students to use the words when they pass you in the hallway by giving out bonus points toward a free-homework pass or toward extra points on a quiz or test.**

- **When a few minutes remain at the end of class, pass out these words on index cards to all students, and have partners use their two specific Tier 2 words to synthesize a part of today's learning.**

See Figures 2.9 and 2.10 for multiple examples of Interactive Academic Word Walls. Teachers in various secondary classrooms created these word walls. Students themselves created some of them, as well. As they designed their own word walls, students made sense of words, phrases, and themes in literature. Vocabulary word chips can be used to learn about shades of meaning and select the most appropriate words to convey a specific meaning (see Figure 2.11).

Figure 2.9 Student-Created Interactive Academic Word Wall

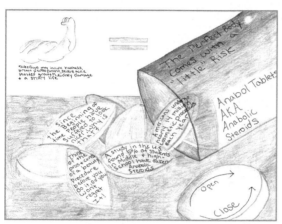

Figure 2.10 Tiered Word Wall to Support English Learners Studying Fables

Figure 2.11 Vocabulary Paint Chips for Shades of Meaning

Many authors and researchers recommend the use of games and partner (or small-group) activities as a way to building robust vocabulary. Isabel Beck et al. (2013), Douglas Fisher and Nancy Frey (2009), Donald Bear and colleagues (2012), as well as Jennifer Cronsberry (2004) and others make the case that vocabulary learning must be interactive and playful, and we agree.

 CHECK THIS OUT

What resources are available to help you choose the word of the day? The best approach is to make this a school-wide effort, or at least to decide on a list in collaboration with your grade-level colleagues. But even if you have to choose these words alone, there are online sources to help you establish target words for the year:

The Academic Word List (Coxhead 2000) (570 headwords): www.victoria.ac.nz/lals /resources/academicwordlist

Academic Word List cross-referenced with simple word families (343 words): http://textproject.org/assets/library/resources/Academic-word-list.pdf

Jim Burke's Academic Vocabulary List (358 words): www.englishcompanion.com /pdfDocs/acvocabulary2.pdf

The Top 60 Most Common Academic Words: www.vocabulary.com/lists/23710

Visual Thesaurus General Academic Vocabulary list: www.visualthesaurus.com /wordlists/144473

Visual Thesaurus VocabGrabber: www.visualthesaurus.com/vocabgrabber

---

Turn-and-Talk

During each lesson, we need to provide multiple opportunities for students to verbally articulate what they are learning. This is one of the most effective ways for students to acquire knowledge. For most learners, simply listening to a teacher talk in front of the room does not provide the processing time necessary to internalize the information. Students need multiple opportunities to explain to their peers what they are learning (Sousa, 2011a). Who does most of the explaining in your classroom? If you answered, "*I do*," you are like most secondary teachers. Instead, try to provide multiple opportunities for students to talk to their peers and make meaning through conversation. For just one to two minutes, have students turn to their preassigned partner (this saves time and minimizes students' complaints about who their partner will be today) to discuss a question you pose or react to a statement you make, such as:

- **Which branch of government is the strongest/most important in your opinion? Cite evidence for your claim.**
- **Based on your knowledge of this character, where do you believe he'll end up ten years from now? Provide reasons for your claim.**

- Interpret this statement: "Population growth is a serious consideration for the future of our global economy."
- Predict what impact this new information/discovery/invention will have in your lifetime?

After this brief turn-and-talk, have a few students share out with the rest of the class.

COACH'S NOTES

Be sure to keep the discussion to only one or two minutes. Engaging your class in this way will ensure thinking on the part of more students than a typical teacher question–student response routine will evoke. In fact, to encourage greater listening skills, ask your students to share out the response that their partner gave them. Soon, you'll find students listening more closely to one another as they enter into these quick conversations.

Stop-and-Jot

Stop-and-jot is an alternative to turn-and-talk. In this brief routine, each student writes for one or two minutes as they reflect upon a teacher-developed question or statement. With the stop-and-jot, you will be preparing more students to participate in the conversation. Once they have had the opportunity to write down their thoughts or comments, they will be more willing to share in a class or small-group discussions. (See Figure 2.12; students jot down their notes in a partially completed graphic organizer and then turn and talk to share their responses with one another.)

Using these two inclusive (i.e., having all students respond at the same time) questioning routines interchangeably requires that *all* students think and respond, encouraging greater student engagement with "minds-on" listening and/or writing. Many more students will be prepared to participate actively in discussion or complete a writing task after engaging in one of these two processing routines.

Figure 2.12 First Students Stop-and-Jot, Then They Turn and Talk

FLEXIBLE GROUPING ROUTINES

As a secondary teacher, you might choose to begin your lesson with whole-class discussions, brainstorms, or minilectures. We agree that whole-group instruction is important, but we also believe that by moving from whole-class activities to flexible groups, you will engage more learners and meet more of their individual needs. In Chapter 1, we addressed flexible grouping for the purpose of community building. Flexible grouping goes beyond building a community of learners; it responds to learners' readiness, interest, and learning profiles.

Carol Ann Tomlinson and Cindy A. Strickland (2005) describe flexible grouping as the "purposeful reordering of students into working groups to ensure that all students work with a wide variety of classmates and in a wider range of contexts during a relatively short span of classroom time" (352). Having students practice the routine of moving back and forth from whole class to small groups (both heterogeneous, as well as homogeneous), to triads, pairs, and individual work arrangements will make transition times smoother and quicker.

Additionally, you can use a Half Class/Half Class (Dodge 2006) structure, where two activities are going on at the same time for between ten and fifteen minutes, and then each half switches to the opposite activity. The novelty of changing up these classroom configurations engages the brain (Jensen 2005). A simple rehearsed movement from whole class into pairs and triads will enable you to quickly vary who does the *explaining* in class. The brief academic conversations that ensue will help learners become more involved.

COACH'S NOTES

I coach teachers on how to deliver a small-group lesson while other groups complete tiered assignments. Some students might work independently, on the computer, and still others receive enrichment and extension activities. Two English language arts teachers with whom I work teach in adjacent classrooms and regularly preassess their students. Then, they combine their classes to form flexible groups based on students' needs (see the following Teacher-2-Teacher). Similarly, math and other content area teachers design learning experiences for their students that require flexible grouping strategies. (See Figures 2.13, 2.14, and 2.15 for students engaged in various grouping configurations in Ms. West's math class.)

Maureen Corio, instructional specialist

Figure 2.13 Flexible Grouping Configuration with Students Working in Larger Groups

Figure 2.14 Flexible Grouping Configuration with Students Working in Smaller Groups

Figure 2.15 Flexible Grouping Configuration with Students Working Independently

Among the many proponents of active learning and kinesthetic experiences in the classroom, Hannaford (2005) made a strong case for movement and physical engagement of learners: "Ninety-five percent of learning occurs through direct, intimate sensory-motor experiences with the environment" (120). When students get out of their seats during class, there is always the potential for noise and distractions; yet, the benefits of learning on their feet have been well documented (Glynn 2001). We suggest that as part of your flexible grouping routines you establish a structure for transitioning and participating in learning processes that require movement.

Teacher-2-Teacher

The Back-to-Back Protocol that we use for pairs of students is really useful because it provides three things that all levels of middle school students benefit from: movement, private thinking time, and recognizing multiple perspectives on a topic. (See Figures 2.16 and 2.17 for photos that show students engaged in this routine.)

Too often, students are afraid to put their ideas "out there" for fear of giving the wrong response. This protocol encourages students to state a position after some private thinking time and try their thinking out on one or more fellow students.

About once a week, I have a series of critical thinking questions prepared regarding the previous night's reading assignment. I ask students to travel around the classroom quietly until I say, "Stop, back-to-back." Students turn back-to-back with another student. The rule is that you can't partner with the same student twice in this activity. Then, I state the question and ask for some private thinking time. After fifteen seconds or so, I say, "Face Time," and students share their ideas while I then listen in on several conversations. I ask the question again to allow for the other student's perspective, and then usually go on to another question. This protocol gets every student involved and allows for all voices to be heard and valued.

Stephanie Brown and Michelle Berger, sixth-grade coteachers of English

Figure 2.16 Sixth-Grade Student Pairs Engaged in the Back-to-Back Protocol During an English Language Arts Class

Figure 2.17 Students Share Ideas During Face Time

Socratic Circles

The *Socratic circle* is often used for whole-class reading instruction. As described on the International Reading Association's ReadWriteThink website (www.readwritethink.org), a Socratic seminar, or a Socratic circle as it is also known, is a formal discussion, based on a text or a work of art, in which the leader asks open-ended questions. Students learn to listen to one another, think critically, and articulate their own thoughts and answers in response to what others have said. Many secondary teachers use the Socratic circle one day a week so that students get used to reading and responding to literature and nonfiction text in an interactive fashion. It promotes academic conversations on the part of students and works well with excerpts of texts, Supreme Court cases, poetry, works of art, and even parts of modules provided by some of the State Education Departments.

This whole-class approach to reading "promotes team building and appropriate classroom behavior. Students are taught to look at one another when they speak and listen, to wait their turn to respond, and to communicate in a way that shows respect for viewpoints differing from their own . . . and, always, to return to the text to find evidence and support for their ideas" (Dodge 2006, 121). Socratic circles provide a powerful routine for engaging students in a close read and analysis of fiction. They also teach students appropriate communication skills while building their background knowledge through the study of content-rich nonfiction.

When using this routine for the first few times, have students create a large circle with chairs (or desks) around the room. Ask each student to write his or her name on a tented index card or piece of folded construction paper. The name cards will add to the formality of the routine, evoking a sense of responsibility to respond to one's peers, rather than just to the teacher. Encourage your students to direct their comments to one another, always using the name of the person to whom they are speaking. For example, one student might say, "I understand what Jared is saying, and I would like to add _____ because on page 3 the author says that _____." Anchor charts with precise academic language and sentence frames for discussion should be displayed in your room so that students can refer to them when participating in this reading routine. Cocreate them with students so they have ownership of the language involved in an exchange of views.

After you have facilitated a whole-class Socratic circle several times, your students can take charge of running their own discussions. You can continue to run the discussion as a whole-class seminar, assigning the facilitation of the conversation to three students at a time. These students will be able to assist one another as leaders. (It will also lessen the impact if one or even two students do not attend class on the day of the seminar.)

Another option is to have students work in small teams to prepare for the discussion. While one small group of students will be involved in the center of the classroom, everyone else will be involved in an outer-circle task. See Figure 2.18 for a list of suggested outer-circle tasks that will keep *all* students on task.

Although there are dozens of ways to run a seminar, the following step-by-step suggestions will help will keep things simple at first:

1. Decide what text students will read. (Will it be a close reading done as a class? Will it be a reading that you have assigned the night before?)
2. Provide a graphic organizer for students to fill in as first they work in small groups to answer text-dependent questions.
3. Be sure that anchor charts around the room list appropriate question starters for clarifying, adding on, and questioning. (Provide a copy of these question starters to each student for individual use.)
4. Decide whether students will . . .
   - start in small groups and then (1) send one representative from their team to debate/discuss the issue in the middle of the classroom or (2) come to the inner circle as a team

Figure 2.18 Outer-Circle Tasks

Following is a suggested list of tasks you can assign randomly or to specific students based on the complexity of the task. You should add additional tasks that you deem important, as well. To simplify some of the tasks, provide a class set of names and/or a graphic organizer on which student can take notes.

- Create a bulleted list of "most important ideas raised" and which students mentioned these ideas.
- Tally how many times the text was quoted by each student.
- Note any tips or hints that students offer when solving a problem.
- Keep track of academic vocabulary used by each participant (refer to anchor charts, word walls, or individual lists of academic vocabulary).
- Keep track of discipline-specific or content-specific vocabulary used by each participant that should pepper the discussion.
- List differences of opinion/multiple perspectives that come up.
- Write the name of student commenting and the perspective he or she holds.
- Record who initiated a new comment, added on to an idea/clarified some confusion, asked a question, or focused on the knowledge or skills of the lesson's objectives.

- replace their representative with a different member of the group, once he or she has spoken twice
- go to a prescribed "hot seat" for a chance to speak, once all members of the team have spoken
- use "talking chips" to encourage participation
- use an inner- and outer-circle format to evaluate each other and have all students in the class engaged.

If you provide students with scaffolds in the form of talking chips, focused tasks, sentence starters, and vocabulary to use, they will be on the way to developing skills to run a discussion on their own.

ThinkTank

When you need to reengage students and encourage deeper processing during a lesson, try a *Think-Tank*. Often, as we get deeper into a lesson, our students' energy plummets (Sousa 2011a), and we may see the need to get students out of their seats or move them into small groups to reengage.

Depending on the size of your class, you might divide it into small groups of four to five students and send them to different areas of the room. At each location, group members brainstorm and record what they know about the same topic (or answer the same question) on chart paper or a dry-erase board.

This collaborative processing routine gets students out of their seats and engages them in very content-focused tasks as they speak, write, and illustrate together. Students make meaning from your lesson as they speak together. Serving as a great prewriting activity, the ThinkTank gives students confidence for their upcoming task. ThinkTanks show students what they know and what they don't know. Three advantages of using the ThinkTank are:

- **It is easy to implement.**
- **It takes only five minutes.**
- **It serves as excellent daily formative assessment.**

SKILL-BUILDING ROUTINES

The need for multiple levels of literacy instruction has been well established. For example, Shanahan and Shanahan (2008) distinguish among (1) *basic literacy*—literacy skills that are crucial for understanding letter–sound correspondence, decoding, and accessing high-frequency words; (2) *intermediate literacy*—skills that are common to many reading tasks and include developing basic fluency when reading, understanding generic academic words and phrases, and applying general comprehension strategies to everyday and academic readings; and (3) *disciplinary literacy*—literacy skills that are essential to understanding and producing text that is unique to each content area, such as literature, history, science, mathematics, music, or any other subject matter.

Fang (2012) reminds us that students must acquire multiple literacy roles to be successful with complex literacy tasks. As *code breakers*, learners access a range of skills and resources to process print and nonprint input (signs, symbols, visual, and graphic representations of information). As *meaning makers*, students interact with the target text and with each other to understand the overall message, to unpack the layers of meaning in the text, and to discover the more subtle implications of the readings. As *text users*, they have regular and meaningful access to a variety of texts written in different genres for different audiences and purposes. As *text analysts and critics*, students critically interpret, analyze, synthesize, and evaluate multiple texts, building upon the scaffolds received from teachers. Because literacy instruction is a complex, multidimensional task that requires various approaches across the content areas, we are selecting routines that will support literacy skill development across the secondary content areas.

Close Reading

Regardless of your content area, close reading is an approach that can be used by any teacher to help students interact with complex texts. It helps them comprehend, analyze, and critique assigned or self-selected readings. One way to encourage close reading is through text annotation. Have students develop their own system for marking up their books, so they can interact with the author and the reading in a more intimate way. Teach text annotations or coding texts to students who might be reluctant to initiate their own system. After you model and students practice using annotations, they will know how to make their thinking visible. There are some standard notation systems available using symbols (see Buehl 2009), or you can make up your own. Color-coding, underlining, or circling text features or using sticky notes will also promote active reading, thinking about the text, and conducting text-level analysis and reflection. Annotating text will prepare students for academic conversations that will follow their independent reading.

NOTE-TAKING ROUTINES

To have students develop independence around note taking, start by developing note-taking skills together. Most secondary teachers expect that their students have already learned how to maintain notebooks and take notes during class discussions and/or PowerPoint Presentations. Inevitably, they are disappointed. Other than being told to *copy* teacher notes from PowerPoint presentations or off the SmartBoard, students are rarely *given instruction* on how to select, organize, and record information. Being able to do this *on their own* is critical to their future success; the notes they take must make sense to them so that the information can be retained, retrieved, and used later on.

Taking notes as a daily practice is rather difficult for most students to master. That students have difficulty with note taking, however, should not surprise us, when we consider that learning to take notes well takes as much time as learning to write in a relatively experienced way (at least fifteen years!) according to Scardamalia and Bereiter (1991). Paying attention to this skill-building activity is crucial because, aside from building organizational skills, notes provide your students with records from which to study. While learning to take notes, your students will also acquire the content-based knowledge of your discipline and build background knowledge.

One way to explicitly teach how to take notes is to *preassess* your students' skills at generating their own notes, and proceed from there. Here's how:

- Give an organized five- to ten-minute lecture and ask students to take notes in the way they prefer. Tell them to keep in mind that these notes will be the only ones from which they can study for an upcoming exam.
- Collect the note-taking samples and sort them into piles of excellent notes, notes that could be improved with a few suggestions, and notes that make little sense to the reader.
- Using a document reader (or reproducing sections of students' notes on a SmartBoard), show the class examples of some of the great note-taking strategies that were used (e.g., skipped lines, boxes or circles used to highlight key vocabulary, enumerated ideas, use of different-colored pens, sketches and diagrams to illuminate concepts, etc.).
- With your class, cocreate an anchor chart titled "Note Takers Do the Following." See Figure 2.19 for an example. It lists ideas like those mentioned above and includes other ideas that your students may decide to add after viewing additional examples. It might include writing questions on the left side of the page and recording details on the right side, itemizing by using bullets, simplifying note taking by using common abbreviations, and so on.
- Once or twice a week, require that students take notes as described above from your daily minilecture.
- Provide five minutes for partners to exchange their notes and decide on one idea to borrow for their next note-taking practice.

Figure 2.19 Anchor Chart on Note Taking: "Note Takers Do the Following"

Note Takers Do the Following:
- ✓ Keep notes brief (use phrases)
- ✓ Put boxes around key vocabulary
- ✓ Circle names of key people, documents events, etc.
- ✓ Underline important information.
- ✓ Number items (enumerate)
- ✓ Use abbreviations
- ✓ Write questions in the margin (that are answered by the notes)
- ✓ Use colored pens/pencils
- ✓ Add drawings, if helpful

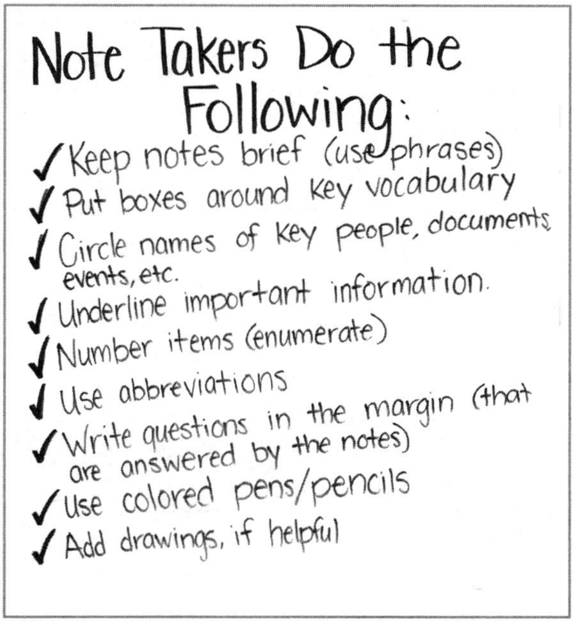

Watch, as over time, student note-taking skills increase and classroom engagement climbs. The end result: improved notes for better studying, heightened pride in students maintaining their own notebooks, increased attention, and greater retention.

Scaffolded Notes

Fearing that students may not note the most important information of a lesson in self-generated notes, you may have begun the school year providing all of your students with scaffolded notes. These guided note-taking sheets provide students with a structure or template they can fill in. After a month or so, try removing some of the scaffolding you have been providing, taking away sentence starters and providing less information in your graphic organizers. As you briefly review students' notes, it will become apparent to you that some students will continue to need the scaffolding.

Column Note Taking

Although we recommend that you begin with scaffolded notes if your students are new to note taking, we also suggest that you soon move on to one of three more engaging structures for note taking. Using Column Note Taking, also known as Cornell Notes (Pauk and Owens 2011), students draw a vertical line down their notebook page, separating the page into two columns (the left side should be about half the size of the right side of the page.) Have them label the wider right side "Notes Column" and the left side "Recall Column." At first, you might scaffold your note takers by providing the left-hand marginal notes (main topics, event, issue, theme, conflict, principle, document, etc.), skipping several lines for students to add their own details, examples, facts, evidence, and so on in the right Notes Column. Struggling learners may continue to need this support as they take notes. It may be difficult for them to listen and take notes at the same time.

Interactive Notebooks

Interactive notebooks can be powerful tools for differentiation. With the growing diversity in classrooms today, you are likely to welcome a tool that addresses these differences.

On the left pages, students take notes gathered from your presentation, text, video, or website. They should be encouraged to write marginal notes on the text (perhaps a nonfictional article provided to them and glued on the left page). On the right pages, students process the meaning of what they are learning by responding, reflecting, making connections, selecting key words, making plans based on the notes or text, noting points of view, or reorganizing the information in a new way.

Teacher-2-Teacher

I decided to use interactive notebooks in my high school Algebra 1A class. This is the first year of a two-year course. One of the benefits is that students will have this notebook for the following year in their second year of algebra. The interactive notebook is used each time we learn a new topic in algebra. It's a great way for students to see what they have learned previously to apply it to newer concepts. I have noticed that the notebook enhances the confidence level in my students because they are proud of their work and use it as a guide when learning new material.

Kaitlin Meyer, algebra teacher

Higher-level thinking should be part of these right-page reflections. According to Susan M. Brookhart (2014), "Higher-order thinking happens when students engage with what they know in such a way as to transform it, and . . . that real knowledge is complex, effortful, generative, evidence-seeking, and reflective" (7). When your students realize that they will be *using their notes* on the left page to craft a response on the right page, they'll make an effort to take better notes.

Some teachers require a table of contents on the first page of the notebook. Keeping pages numbered helps students with organizational skills. The reference to teacher input (left page) and student output (right page) will remind you to provide time for students to process. Because this notebook is somewhat limited in pages, many teachers have chosen to use it as a summary note-taking experience on Fridays as a review of the week. They use a second notebook for daily (usually more plentiful) notes and keep these interactive notebooks (for summary notes) in their rooms. A notebook crafted in this way can serve as a great study tool for an end-of-year review. See Figure 2.20 for a set of guidelines on how to develop an interactive notebook with your class.

Figure 2.20 Guidelines for Developing an Interactive Notebook

Guidelines for Developing an Interactive Notebook

Interactive Note Taking

The interactive notebook will have a left-side, right-side orientation.

The first page(s) of the notebook will contain the table of contents.

All pages will be numbered from left to right: 1, 1A, 2, 2A, 3, 3A, and so on.

Left Pages (Teacher Input)	Right Pages (Student Output and Engagement)
Notes gathered from video, PowerPoint, or Internet site	Integration of terms/content to process for long-term memory
Note taking: class notes or text notes	Evidence of student processing
List of terms, definitions, content	Questioning of the text—students generate their own questions
Content information/reading/text provided by the teacher	Use of higher-order skills to make meaning from information
Charts, maps, documents, graphic organizers provided by teacher	Student reflections, connections, evaluations, reorganization of information, illustrations (option: can be done as homework)
Informational articles provided by teacher	Charts, maps, graphic organizers created by the student

Request that students bring the following materials to class and store:

Colored pens

Colored pencils and highlighters

Glue stick or roll of tape

A pad of sticky notes

Assessments:

Notebooks will be collected and graded periodically.

A class-developed rubric will be used for evaluation.

Assessment criteria will include organization, connections made, thoroughness, and neatness/visual appeal.

Adapted with permission from *History Alive! Interactive Student Notebook Manual,* TCI (1999), www.teachtci.com

Dialectical Journals

As you continue to stretch your students toward greater independence with note taking, consider dialectical journals. These conversations between the reader and the text, often called *double-entry journals*, serve as a sophisticated way for readers to interact with text.

Dividing their page in two equal columns, your students will copy phrases or passages of text that are powerful, confusing, moving, full of irony or foreshadowing, and so on in the left column. They'll record the quote and page where it is found. In the right column, they will respond with their own thoughts, reflections, connections, and insights. You can scaffold by providing the quotes for them in the left margin. They can practice responding to your quotes, until you feel they are ready to choose their own passages for analysis and reflection. Some students will probably need this scaffolding longer than others as this type of note taking may be too abstract for some struggling learners to use independently. See Figure 2.21 for an sample of an eleventh-grade student's English notes taken in the form of a dialectical journal. As you stretch your students toward greater independence with note taking, they will be able to take this critical strategy with them to college.

Figure 2.21 An Example of a Dialectical Journal on *Night* by Elie Wiesel

DIALECTICAL JOURNAL

NAME: Ben   DATE: _____

READING: Night by Elie Wiesel

QUOTE	MY RESPONSE
"Never shall I forget that night, the first night in camp, which has turned my life into one long night seven times cursed and seven times sealed" pg 44	I feel that this statement captures each Holocaust survivor's plight, the inability to move past the horrors of the concentration camps.
"Where is God? Where is He?" pg 9	This question is still being asked in response to the Holocaust. The voice cried out "If he really is what he is, why didn't he do something?"
"I heard a Jew behind me heave a sigh," "What can we expect?" he said. "It's war."	The same inactivity, compliance, and naievety displayed here is exactly what allowed Hitler to gain power in the first place.

End-of-Class Routines

At the end of class, you may be inclined to summarize the day's lesson. However, presenting this lesson review yourself, *instead* of providing students with *their own routine* for closure, contributes little to enhancing their memory (Sousa 2011a; 2011b). Sousa recommends that closure not be conducted as a *teacher's oral review* but, rather, with students' brains fully engaged. If you want to give an oral review, he suggests you do so *before* closure. The best closure routines occur when students actively participate in the synthesis of their own knowledge.

Before students leave your class, you should ask yourself, "How do I know they know?" to determine whether or not today's Learning Targets have been met. There are many routines for bringing closure to a lesson.

LESSON SUMMARY AND REFLECTION ROUTINES

Although formative assessments are discussed here as a routine used to end a lesson, formative assessment also takes place at the beginning or middle of the lesson. If you make summaries, reflections, observations, and conferences part of your instructional repertoire, you will support the learning process in your classroom and lead students down the road to mastery. Some useful tools for formative assessment include choice exit cards and academic journals or learning logs.

Exit and Choice Exit Cards

Many teachers have used exit cards to wind up their lessons and assess their learners. These short summaries, explanations, problems solved, or responses to a teacher-provided prompt serve as evidence of what each child has learned that day. Used to its full advantage, exit cards should guide tomorrow's instruction. Offer appropriately leveled activities to address the different needs of your students. You don't need to use exit cards daily for all of your classes. Instead, try to do one exit card per week with each of your classes. Exit cards should not be graded; it takes only take five minutes to sort them into levels of understanding acquired by students and to provide you with an overall assessment of your class.

Have you ever used a *choice* exit card with students? These creative alternatives address the needs of diverse learners. (See Figure 2.22 and Figure 2.23 for examples of completed choice exit cards by students in an English class and a physics class.) Choices might include summarizing today's lesson through illustrations with captions, creating a bulleted list of examples, making a connection from today's learning to a previously learned topic, or writing a summary paragraph that includes teacher-selected vocabulary terms from a word wall.

Academic Journals/Learning Logs

Another routine for bringing closure to your lesson is to have students make an entry in an academic journal or learning log. This summarizing routine gives students time to stake a claim and provide supporting evidence, make an observation and elaborate with details, note an important connection (such as a comparison, a cause and effect, or a sequence of events or steps), or solve

Figure 2.22 Completed English Choice Exit Card

Name: __Jillian__ Period: ____
Date: ____ Topic: Short Story by Richard Connell

The Most Dangerous Game

In this story, an arrogant hunter goes on a journey to the Amazon to hunt jaguars. During the trip, rocky waves knock him overboard and carry him to an unknown island. He stumbles upon a man living in a mansion and is forced to participate in a manhunt. While fighting for his life he learned to never underestimate his opponent and to respect life. He was a hunter that became the huntee.

Create a bulleted list of ideas
Write a summary
Picture What I've Learned (illustrate with captions)
Make-a-Connection! (describe cause-effect, problem-solution, compare-contrast, sequence, change over time, future implications, etc.)
Argue why this information is important to know about

Figure 2.23 Completed Physics Choice Exit Card

Name: __Jared__ Period: ____
Date: ____ Topic: Physics: Newton's 3rd law

When you punch a wall, the wall exerts the same force back at your hand.

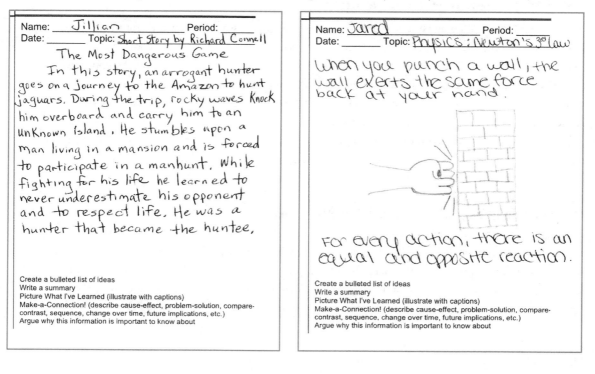

For every action, there is an equal and opposite reaction.

Create a bulleted list of ideas
Write a summary
Picture What I've Learned (illustrate with captions)
Make-a-Connection! (describe cause-effect, problem-solution, compare-contrast, sequence, change over time, future implications, etc.)
Argue why this information is important to know about

CHECK THIS OUT

See these resources to improve your practice of formative assessment:

Centre for Educational Research and Innovation. 2005. *Formative Assessment: Improving Learning in Secondary Classrooms.* Paris: OECD.

Chappuis, J., R. J. Stiggins, S. Chappuis, and J. A. Arter. 2011. *Classroom Assessment for Student Learning: Doing It Right—Using It Well,* 2d ed. Upper Saddle River, NJ: Pearson.

Dodge, J. 2009. *25 Quick Formative Assessments for a Differentiated Classroom.* New York: Scholastic.

Frey, N., and D. Fisher. 2011. *The Formative Assessment Action Plan: Practical Steps to More Successful Teaching and Learning.* Alexandria, VA: ASCD.

Popham, W. J. 2008. *Transformative Assessment.* Alexandria, VA: ASCD.

Various authors. 2014. "Using Assessments Thoughtfully." Special Issue, *Educational Leadership* 71 (6).

Wiliam, D. 2011. *Embedded Formative Assessment.* Bloomington, IN: Solution Tree Press.

and analyze an exemplar problem of the week. Some teachers use it daily. Others prefer to use the academic journal or learning log once a week to have their students sum up what they have learned, to evaluate their performance this week, and to set goals for next week. Consider the questions in Figure 2.24 as a scaffolding tool for self-reflection.

Figure 2.24 Questions for Self-Evaluation and Goal Setting

Have I participated in most classroom discussions?

Have I used the academic words we've discussed in my responses?

Have I taken notes with the guidelines we have covered in class?

Have I completed all assigned written homework?

Have I read all assigned reading at home?

Next week, I plan to work on . . .

Although time may not allow you to collect an exit card each day, you can maximize the likelihood that a greater number of students will take away meaning from today's lesson if you implement a reflection routine, as often as possible, at the end of class. Providing such a *Three-Minute Pause* (Buehl 2001) will invite students to reflect on what they've learned and make a plan for how they can improve their process for learning.

Special Considerations

Certainly, you will find that not every routine recommended in this chapter will work the same way with every class. Instead, use your "instructional intelligence" and the suggestions that follow to modify the routines for special situations, such as having more than one hundred students, teaching multiple courses, sharing classrooms, having longer class periods, or desiring to use more technology.

What if you teach over 100 students each day?

You'll want to teach your students to take charge of facilitating their own learning using flexible groups, passing out and collecting their own materials, and learning routines to check one another's homework. The harder your students work at these routines, the easier it will be for you to manage the volume of learners that you have.

What if you teach multiple courses each semester?

Establish a routine for designing your lesson plans so that each instructional period follows a predictable format. Although this may cut down on the organic nature of teaching different groups of learners, once these routines are comfortably in place, you will be able to be more spontaneous. If you teach several different courses, this will make designing your curriculum plans easier.

Cocreate *generic* anchor charts that can be used with multiple classes and/or grade levels. Charts that scaffold academic conversations, help students generate their own questions, or remind classes how to engage in a particular practice can be used for any course or grade level. This will simplify your day-to-day management of different courses.

What if you don't have your own classroom?

Design your lessons by storing all the necessary documents, such as lesson plans, PowerPoints, video clips, Web links, and handouts in the Cloud. Even if you have to travel from classroom to classroom, you will have easy access to all your teacher-created resources and digital materials on the Web.

George Layer and Michelle Gural's portable student word walls were created out of necessity for their high school algebra classes (see Figure 2.25). They taught in so many different classrooms that establishing a permanent word wall in each one was next to impossible. Instead, they designed word walls that students would bring to each class in their notebooks.

Figure 2.25 Portable Student Word Walls

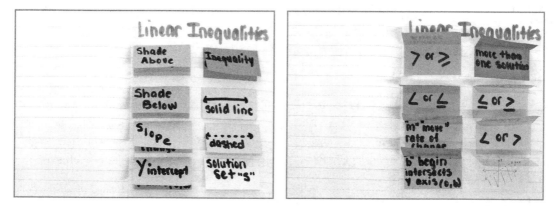

What if your class period is longer than the typical forty- to forty-four-minute class?

With the extra time that you have, you will be able to present information in multiple formats and to select numerous processing routines so that information is accessible to a larger number of students. There will be additional time for you to try out different literacy skill-building suggestions made in this chapter. Experiment with multiple note-taking routines so students can use laptops, iPads, and other digital devices to select, organize, and record information. Designate additional class time for working in interactive notebooks so students become more engaged in their learning process. Use Socratic circles more than once a week so that students have increased practice with facilitating academic conversations.

What if you want to incorporate technology?

Let the big ideas of your content and curriculum drive the technology. If there are ways to enhance the learning process by taking virtual field trips, seeing simulations, publishing to a global audience, or participating in an international technology project, they should be used, if possible. See www.educatorstechnology.com for the latest on using educational Web tools and mobile Apps to enhance your classroom.

Teacher-2-Teacher

Using online surveys (such as polleverywhere.com) can show student learning during a single period or a longer lesson. I have students answer a few quick questions using an online survey as a Do-Now or Daily Warm-up. We analyze the class data and proceed with the lesson. At the conclusion, students take the same or similar survey again and compare the data to the original survey. Students are excited to share their opinions and know that their "vote" counts. Incorporating surveys allows students to see learning taking place in the classroom as responses from the first and second survey differ.

Jeff M. Jakob, National Board–certified teacher and social studies instructional coach

A Final Thought

The routines you put in place daily will help your students know what to expect. By focusing students with Learning Targets, essential questions, and Do-Nows, you'll hook them at the beginning of your lesson. Over time, you'll help them generate their own questions, drawing them further into their own personal learning experiences. During class, encourage students to read closely, make meaning through brief conversations with peers, and take notes in ways that enhance their critical thinking and independence. As it moves from whole class, to small groups, to triads and pairs, your community of learners will continue to grow and have their needs met through flexible-grouping routines. End-of-lesson summary routines and brief formative assessments will help students embed the day's learning and show you and them how far they've come. The routines described in this chapter are best practices from which you can choose, making every day a productive one. When students know that "this is the way we do things around here," everyone benefits.

Essential Questions for Individual Reflection, Collegial Circles, and Group Discussions

- *How does using routines help students at the beginning, middle, and end of each lesson?*

- *Which three routines will you add to your existing practice? What will each of these new routines offer to you and your students?*

- *Which routines would you choose to support John Hattie's (2012) quote, "Teachers and students need to know the learning intentions and the criteria for student success for their lessons" (19)?*

- *Which routines would you use to help students become more self-directed and independent learners?*

- *How can you integrate academic vocabulary routines into your daily instruction?*

- *Are there any additional routines you have used successfully and would share with your colleagues?*

Knowing the answers will help you in school. Knowing how to question will help you in life.

Warren Berger, *A More Beautiful Question*

Education is something other people do to you, whereas LEARNING is what you do to yourself.

Joichi Ito

Chapter **3**

BEGINNING-, MIDDLE-, AND END-OF-UNIT ROUTINES

Overview

In this chapter, we

- summarize research support for the routines we present
- establish routines for the beginning, middle, and end of a unit
- present examples, templates, resources, and classroom vignettes along with recommendations from coaches to support the implementation of unit routines
- discuss special considerations for variations in teaching assignments (large number of students, multiple courses or multiple sections of the same course, varied lengths of class periods, technology integration).

Beginning-, Middle-, and End-of-Unit Routines at a Glance

ROUTINE 1 --→ **Beginning-of-Unit Routines**
- Anticipation Guide
- Virtual Exploration

ROUTINE 2 --→ **Middle-of-Unit Routines**
- Meaning-Making Routines
  - Making Arguments
  - S-O-S
  - Exhibition
- Academic Language Routines
  - Word-Level
  - Sentence-Level
  - Text-Level
  - Talk-About
- Homework Routines
  - Choice Homework Night
  - Foldable

ROUTINE 3 --→ **End-of-Unit Routines**
- Collaborative Review Routines
  - Alphabet Round-Up
  - ThinkTank
  - Stations
  - Text Talk
  - MathChat!

What Does the Research Say About Designing Instructional Units?

When Doug Fisher and Nancy Frey (2008) describe effective instruction, they suggest that we "teach with the learning cycle in mind, using an instructional framework that supports how humans learn" (21). Their structured model for teaching (Fisher and Frey 2008), based on the gradual release of responsibility model of comprehension (Pearson and Gallagher 1983), can help guide you to more strategically plan your units. Within a unit of study, specially designed lessons should activate and build background knowledge throughout each phase of instruction and include the following elements:

- *a focus lesson,* where the teacher establishes a purpose, models actions or processes, and conducts think-alouds
- *guided instruction,* where the teacher uses cues, prompts, and questions to scaffold learner comprehension
- *collaborative learning,* where students work with partners or in small groups to synthesize background knowledge with new learning
- *independent learning,* where students use what they have learned—now part of their background knowledge—in a new way or continue to build background knowledge by reading or researching further.

In reality, these phases of instruction may play out over two to three days, as students work together or engage in independent research. Fisher and Frey remind us that the phases are not necessarily implemented in lockstep but, rather, in any sequence necessary to build the background knowledge needed by your learners.

Historically, the most widely applied framework for instructive lesson design has been Madeline Hunter's Elements of Lesson Design (1984). Although she warned against the expectation that all elements must be observed in every lesson (Costa 1984, as cited in Marzano 2003), supervisors rigidly checked off each element during teacher observations. To allow for more flexibility, Benjamin Bloom (1976) suggested that instead of using these elements for individual lesson design, we look to see how they fit into a framework for units. More recently, unit design has focused on Backwards Design (Wiggins and McTighe 1998, 2005), where teachers start with the end in mind (the desired results), determine acceptable evidence needed to document the desired learning, and then plan the instructional activities and curriculum to get there. This task analysis is the reverse of what has so long determined curriculum unit design—textbooks, favorite lessons of teachers, and time-honored activities. By looking to employ these research-based strategies over the course of a unit, we are less constrained as we plan our daily lessons.

Routines for the Beginning, Middle, and End of a Unit

We recognize that, just like a lesson, a *beginning, a middle,* and *an end* can frame every unit. *At the beginning of each unit,* you will use routines to help you activate, assess, and build your students' background knowledge. These routines will build curiosity, promote interest, inspire new learning, and help your students link this new unit of study to what they already know. During the middle of the unit, you will focus on routines that expand concept attainment, skill building, and academic language development. A unit of instruction should end with routines that allow your students to review and consolidate their new learning as well as for you to assess student progress with the target content and skills.

ROUTINE 1 — Beginning-of-Unit Routines

As documented by research—as well as evidenced by successful classroom practices—routines for *activating, assessing,* and *building* background knowledge are necessary for good instruction. Although there are many ways to engage with background knowledge, the first commitment you must make is to regularly create opportunities to activate, assess, and build background knowledge *as you begin each new unit.*

COACH'S NOTES

You may be wondering, "Where am I going to find the time to add routines for building background knowledge, when I barely have enough time to cover my curriculum content?" Being aware of the research, however, we cannot deny the importance of activating and building background knowledge. Because of time constraints, we must be more strategic in our lesson planning. Keep in mind that activating and building background knowledge helps your students remember more of your content.

ANTICIPATION GUIDE

Anticipation guides—also referred to as *anticipatory guides*—help teachers activate prior knowledge, validate students' existing understandings, and preview new material. They also help identify misconceptions and gaps in students' knowledge. Additionally, anticipation guides build curiosity and stimulate student interest in the forthcoming reading (Duffelmeyer 1994; Wood et al. 2008). Figure 3.1 is an example of what an anticipation guide looks like when the purpose is to introduce a new unit on World War I. Figure 3.2 is a student example of an anticipation guide completed before and after reading an article about spelling in the English language. Anticipation guides are unique in the sense that they help bridge all three phases of working with background knowledge, thus scaffolding learning in multiple ways:

- They *assess* prior knowledge by having students evaluate a teacher-provided list of statements about the topic.
- They *activate* what students already know and make apparent the misconceptions that some students hold.
- They *build* background in several ways: They preview key concepts and introduce vocabulary prior to reading; they provide a purpose for reading; they help students integrate and consolidate new learnings.

See the companion website at heinemann.com/products/E07434.aspx for a blank template that you can use to design your own anticipation guide.

Figure 3.1 Anticipation Guide Designed for a Unit on World War I

Before Reading (Agree or Disagree?)	Statements	After Reading (Agree or Disagree?)	After Reading (Evidence Found in Text)
	1. World War I resolved all major conflicts in Europe.		
	2. The United States was a well-respected member of the League of Nations.		
	3. Britain, France, and Italy wanted to punish Germany for causing the war.		
	4. The Bolshevik revolution was a direct result of World War I.		
	5. Some of the new weapons utilized during World War I are still used today and include machine guns, tanks, planes, and nuclear weapons.		
	6. The sinking of the *Lusitania* and unrestricted submarine warfare prompted the United States to join the Allied powers in World War I.		
	7. The Axis powers during World War I included Germany, Italy, Hungary, and Japan.		

Wonder Questions:

Figure 3.2 Anticipation Guide for a Nonfiction Article on English Spelling

Name _Megan_

Anticipation Guide

Topic/Article/Story: <u>"English Spelling Is Confusing, but a Language Group Says</u>
<u>It Can Fix That" by Chicago Tribune, adapted by Newsela</u>

Before Reading (Agree or Disagree?)	Statements	After Reading (Agree or Disagree?)
Agree	1. English spelling is confusing.	Agree
Agree	2. The International English Spelling Congress should come up with a spelling system that makes more sense.	disagree
Disagree	3. There is no correlation between how words are written and how they sound.	Disagree
Disagree	4. Language experts should propose a list of new spelling to correct problem word groups.	Agree
Agree	5. Congress should select an alternate spelling system.	disagree

Summary Statement:

Before I read this I thought _That the English language_
is Confusing,

but now I know _that I still think it is confusing_
but changing it might not be for the best

We recently visited a classroom where every student was completely engaged as they were observing, measuring, collecting, and analyzing data and summarizing what they had learned. What made this class so dynamic? The teacher stopped the minilesson and said, "We're going on a field trip!" Students quickly scattered to tanks of small sea animals. We immediately thought any teacher could evoke similar enthusiasm by creating a classroom routine of "going on a field trip." However, most schools don't have this kind of equipment or enough money to go on actual field trips, so we thought about ways to make "field trips" virtual. Most schools are moving toward equipping their schools with additional technology, so virtual "field trips" will become increasingly more available to teachers and their students.

Teacher-2-Teacher

I launch each unit with a Thorny Statements fishbowl discussion. The purpose of these discussions is to introduce the themes, conflicts, and essential questions that my students will encounter/explore throughout the unit. The students in the fishbowl respond to controversial statements that connect to the unit's content. Students are encouraged to make claims and cite their prior knowledge as supporting evidence. Students in the outer circle provide their inner-circle partners with discussion feedback. I differentiate this exercise by allowing my highly verbal students to participate in the inner circle and my introverted students to participate from the outer circle. Students who need more wait time benefit from observing from the outer circle and providing focused, written feedback to their inner-circle partners.

I launched my Individuality and Conformity unit with the following "thorny" statements: "It is better to fit in than to stand out," "Attractive models and remarkable athletes make everyone else feel insecure; they shouldn't be allowed to flaunt their talents," and "Kids should be loyal to their friends even if it puts their own well-being at risk." These statements immediately hooked my students and gave them an authentic purpose to critically analyze our unit readings: Kurt Vonnegut's "Harrison Bergeron," Evan Hunter's "The Last Spin," and Todd Strasser's "On the Bridge."

Alex Corbitt, seventh-grade English teacher

VIRTUAL EXPLORATION

A virtual approach to building background knowledge helps infuse technology into the twenty-first-century curriculum; it also just might become one of your students' favorite ways to learn.

As you're planning your unit, think about what prior knowledge would help your learners make meaning of the key understandings. If you are studying geography and landforms and how they impact the development of a civilization and your students have never been far away from their community, it's time to take a virtual field trip to Greece or China. If your students have never seen amphibians or reptiles up close, it's time to take a virtual field trip to a zoo. If you are comparing the branches of the U.S. government and your students have never been to Washington, DC, it's time to take a virtual field trip to the capital. If you're discussing the effects of hurricanes and other destructive weather events, it's time to take a virtual field trip *into* one of them. If you are teaching students to use the Pythagorean theorem, "take" them to real landmarks around the world and have them determine the shadow they each cast upon the ground with the measurement details you provide.

Teacher-2-Teacher

Integrating Skype in the classroom provides real-world application of skills that teach students how to communicate effectively, generate thoughtful, evidence-based questions, and hold a sustained academic discussion. (See Figure 3.3 for how students are engaged to interact with others via Skype.) There are several different ways that you can integrate Skype across curricula, including playing the popular Mystery Skype game or connecting with other teachers to share a lesson or host a presentation. For teachers who participate in Mystery Skype, two classrooms come together from anywhere in the world and use yes-or-no questions, combined with evidence gathered from answers, to narrow down the location. The students also use geographical and research tools throughout the process, logging the "facts learned" and using them to guide their process. Other Skype lessons are more transparent and focus on connecting classrooms globally using Skype as a discussion and collaboration platform. Regardless of the lesson, Skype opens the door in any classroom for an authentic learning experience, where students are exposed to study skills, content, and cultures in a fun, challenging way!

Nicole A. Long, seventh-grade English language arts teacher
http://mrslongsclassroomskype.weebly.com

Figure 3.3 Students Trying to Identify the Mystery Skype Callers' Location

During each unit, provide many opportunities for small-group explorations of the target content and skills via *academic conversations* so that students may build their academic language and use it to make connections among key ideas, essential understandings, and skills. In addition to helping your students build content skills, the routines you choose throughout the unit should help students make connections, persuade others, and create visual representations and oral summaries of the learning that takes place in your classroom.

MEANING-MAKING ROUTINES

The meaning-making routines that you choose should help students uncover the essence and nuances of your unit. They should invite students to contemplate, make connections, stake a claim, and share information with others. Once you've set the stage for your new unit by using anticipation guides and taking virtual field trips, you are ready for the "meat and potatoes" of the unit and for helping students make sense of it.

Making Arguments

Writing is so important to successful learning that we urge you to make a commitment to integrate writing into your classroom on a *daily* basis. Writing freewrites, directed freewrites, summaries, entries in learning logs, and opinions in personal journals, all help us to *see what we think*. Once we get something down on paper, we can understand an idea more clearly and deal with it more tangibly. Although narrative writing, informative/explanatory writing, and argument are all important for students to be successful in school, by the time students reach secondary school, argument writing becomes of paramount importance.

Vicky Giouroukakis and Maureen Connolly (2012) aptly described why argument writing is crucial to student learning: "How else will they be able to convince their professor that they deserve a higher grade in the course; or their employer that they deserve a raise; or their local councilman that building nuclear power plants in their neighborhood will increase the risk of cancer and other diseases and endanger people's lives?" (65).

The ability to stake a claim in an analysis of topics or texts using valid reasoning and relevant and sufficient evidence is not an easy skill for students to develop, but develop it they must. Writing an argument proficiently takes years of practice, and, for that reason, we support a scaffolded approach throughout the years and across the disciplines that focuses on argument as a key type of writing in every classroom.

S-O-S

To scaffold argument writing, we suggest you use one of the S-O-S Summary templates shown below (adapted from Dodge [2009]). These simple-to-use documents provide you with multiple opportunities to have students express the opinion of the author and provide evidence from that text, *without having to write a full essay*. Taking no more than ten minutes to complete, the S-O-S scaffolds the thinking necessary to write an argument essay, without demanding the linguistic format that is usually required to complete it.

Ask students to read a *statement* that you provide, and analyze it with the help of a recently studied text (speech, magazine article, news report, current events article, etc.) or pair of texts. Have them choose one article (or one of two sides of an issue presented within the same article), state the author's *opinion* (position, point of view, or claim), and create a bulleted list of evidence to *support* this viewpoint. The S-O-S can be assigned for homework in preparation for a brief debate to be held the next day.

Bringing their completed S-O-S with them to one side of the classroom, students will argue for or against your provided statement. Some examples:

- **Hydrogen fuel cells will be the best source of energy for the future.**
- **Fracking is not dangerous to our environment.**
- **Genetically modified foods are safe for consumption.**
- **Biographies give us more accurate insight into a person's life than do autobiographies.**
- **Roman legacies have left a greater impact on our society than did the contributions of the Greeks.**
- **Our government should be not allowed to uncover personal information via social media.**

After students debate and listen to multiple viewpoints, you can make this routine more rigorous. Students can write an argument expressing the opposing viewpoint. Using this S-O-S routine regularly with students (once or twice a unit) will prepare them to participate in the kind of argument and debates they are likely to find in future college classrooms or local community meetings.

Below is an example of an S-O-S Summary prompt for a sixth-grade science classroom. Keep in mind that you should provide the prompt in the form of a *statement*, not a *question* ("The periodic table of elements is not organized very well" not, "Is the periodic table of elements organized well or poorly?"). This format scaffolds students by providing them a routine to practice responding to *a claim*, agreeing or disagreeing, and providing two to three pieces of evidence for support. See Figure 3.4 for the S-O-S Summary that was assigned by this science teacher and Figure 3.5 for an adapted S-O-S Summary sketch completed during a class in the library.

Teacher-2-Teacher

I used the S-O-S Summary during our chemistry unit for a quick check of the students' knowledge of the periodic table. On the board I wrote the statement, "The periodic table of elements is not organized very well." My students could agree or disagree but had to come up with three facts to back up their opinion. Some students thought the table was very unorganized and confusing, but when I asked them to show me evidence of this disorganization, they really couldn't.

Before we started our unit on the periodic table, the table did look a little intimidating and confusing, but while we were learning about it, students caught on. For next year, I think I will use this S-O-S before we learn about the periodic table, and then again, after the unit is over.

Mary Andrade, middle school science teacher

Exhibition

At the beginning of a new unit, place a blank time line or blank piece of mural paper around your room to provide learners with a visual repository for making sense of information, as it is uncovered throughout the unit. Annotated visuals that students should be required to create will help them make comparisons, note cause and effect, point out a sequence, and observe change over time throughout any unit. Visuals will help all of your learners but most especially your English language learners.

Once you've laid out the blank poster paper or blank time line around your room, your job will be done, and your students' work should begin. The best visuals are those that are created by the students themselves, not premade posters purchased in a teachers' store. Encourage students to sign up for the beginning, middle, or end of the unit, and ask them to bring *at least two artifacts* to add to the exhibition during that phase of the unit. Each artifact posted in the exhibit might be accompanied by a brief caption written below on an index card. The two artifacts could be assigned as homework or equal to a quiz grade for the unit. By having students sign up for different sections of the unit, you can make sure all subtopics will be covered in the final exhibition.

Alternately, small groups can be assigned a section of the unit and they can complete the exhibition routine at the end of the unit. See Figure 3.6 for suggestions on what types of artifacts can be collected and displayed across the content areas.

Figure 3.4 S-O-S Summary on the Periodic Table of Elements

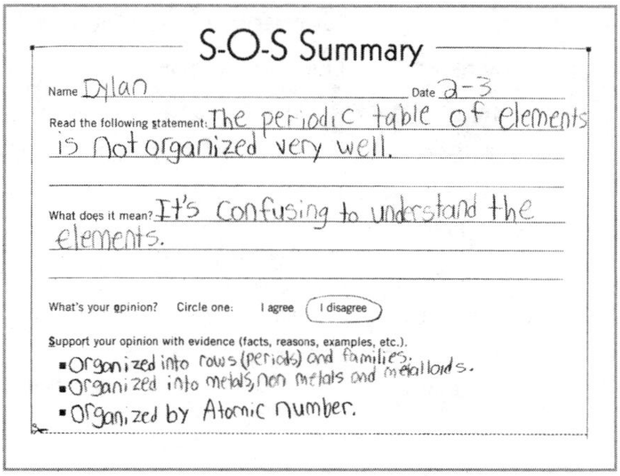
S-O-S Summary

Name Dylan Date 2-3

Read the following statement: The periodic table of elements is not organized very well.

What does it mean? It's confusing to understand the elements.

What's your opinion? Circle one: I agree (I disagree)

Support your opinion with evidence (facts, reasons, examples, etc.).

- Organized into rows (periods) and families.
- Organized into metals, non metals and metalloids.
- Organized by Atomic number.

Figure 3.5 S-O-S Summary Sketch on an Informational Text

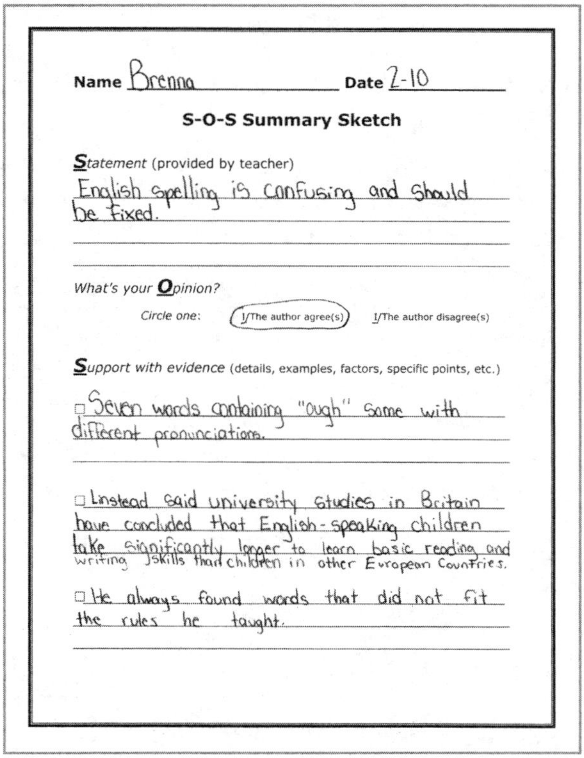
Name Brenna Date 2-10

S-O-S Summary Sketch

Statement (provided by teacher)

English spelling is confusing and should be fixed.

What's your Opinion?

Circle one: (I/The author agree(s)) I/The author disagree(s)

Support with evidence (details, examples, factors, specific points, etc.)

□ Seven words containing "ough" some with different pronunciations.

□ Linstead said university studies in Britain have concluded that English-speaking children take significantly longer to learn basic reading and writing skills than children in other European Countries.

□ He always found words that did not fit the rules he taught.

Figure 3.6 Artifacts for Exhibitions Across the Content Areas

Artifacts in a social studies classroom exhibition might include:

- A downloaded and highlighted map
- A hand-drawn book cover
- A drawn symbol (of the conflict, theme, etc.)
- An actual artifact (a coin, a model, etc.)
- A sketch/illustration
- A primary source
- A photo/sketch of a significant person
- A set of headlines (showing two points of view)
- Artwork from the time period
- A "quote"
- A secondary source
- A re-created document
- Key terms used at the time

Artifacts in a math classroom exhibition might include:

- Real-world applications
- Different types of graphs
- Multiple representations for the same ____
- Examples of when to use the concept
- A calculator or other math tools
- Key terms (to be understood)
- Illustrations/sketches/nonlinguistic representations
- Manipulatives

Artifacts in an English classroom exhibition might include:

- A sketch
- A "quote"
- A drawn map of the setting
- Symbolic pictures that represent the theme
- Symbols for events
- A symbolic drawing of the conflict
- A list of attributes that describe the protagonist
- Textual evidence about the theme

Artifacts in a science classroom exhibition might include:

- Multiple examples of ____
- A drawing or sketch
- An illustration of the concept *in action*
- Multiple graphs/charts/or maps
- A sequence of steps
- Famous scientists and their contributions
- Tools or equipment to be used
- Listed parts and functions of ____
- Listed cause–effect relationships

Teacher-2-Teacher

My art class time line was inspired by what I felt was a lack of context in the delivery of instruction with art projects. To create a better structure, I wrote a plan for grades 7 (realism) and grade 8 (expressionism) to follow a time line of the historical art movements as they relate to relevant historical events.

ACADEMIC LANGUAGE ROUTINES

Academic language helps all students master curriculum content. It is the type of abstract and cognitively demanding language students must acquire in school. It will help them understand new concepts and the complex information presented in the content areas as well as the ability to recognize and apply how language is used in each discipline. Internalizing academic language is more than just learning challenging vocabulary; it also leads to forming more sophisticated sentences and understanding and producing more complex texts. For this reason, we suggest implementing the word-level, sentence-level, and text-level routines with your students.

Word-Level

Most teachers spend some instructional time on the teaching of vocabulary. However, it varies from class to class how words are selected and which methods are used to either directly or indirectly teach them. Here are some examples of the types of words that foster academic language proficiency:

- discipline-specific vocabulary: *density, filibuster, and ratio*
- cross-disciplinary words: *analyze, interpret, sequence*
- *phrases* and idiomatic expressions *that are discipline-specific (conservation of energy* and *greatest common factor)* as well as cross-disciplinary (*text-based evidence).*

When addressing word-level academic language, consider an approach to vocabulary teaching suggested by Robert Marzano and Julia Simms (2013):

1. Offer a clear explanation or student-friendly description.
2. Have students restate the definition or example in their own words.
3. Make sure students create a graphic representation for words.
4. Engage students in varied, motivating activities with the words.
5. Create opportunities for students to discuss target vocabulary.
6. Introduce students to gamelike activities that invite them to use new words.

Consider one or more word-level routines to be used regularly in each unit, such as building academic word walls, having students maintain a content-specific dictionary, illustrated glossary, or word study book, or playing vocabulary games to review and practice key terms. See Figure 3.7 for a word wall built by Christine Pearsall and Anne Logan posted in the hallway of a middle school. The QR codes give hints such as photos or video clips for the meaning of the Tier 2 words that appear frequently across the grade levels and content areas. The word walls are updated regularly for increased student engagement around the building.

Sentence-Level

The idea of examining text at the sentence level might be new for many teachers. Yet, sentence-level work is essential if we want to help students comprehend complex texts and be able to string together words into meaningful sentences. If your students have difficulties with forming complex sentences,

Figure 3.7 Vocabulary on the Go

help them see how words are combined in meaningful ways. See Figure 3.8 for Michele Diaz's anchor chart that supports more complex academic language use.

Figure 3.8 Anchor Chart That Supports Academic Language Use

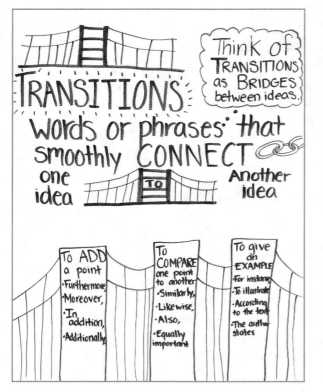

In addition to anchor charts, try the following approach:

Set aside five to ten minutes of instruction from time to time to offer students a guided exploration of a carefully selected, complex sentence unique to your discipline. This practice, also called *sentence dissection* (Honigsfeld and Dove 2013) or sentence cross-examination (Dodge and Honigsfeld 2014), is best if the excerpt comes from a text used for literacy or content-based instruction, such as a textbook, a scholarly article or essay, a piece of literature or even a released standardized test question.

During this structured session devoted to sentence cross-examination, take your students through a guided exploration or cross-examination of the target sentence both for meaning and logistic/grammatical form. Lily Wong Fillmore (2012) reminds us that students need a preplanned instructional conversation and engagement in "discussion focused on various aspects of a sentence or two chosen . . . for their grammatical features or complexity" (10). The sentence should be rich in information as well as opportunities for discussing word choice, phrases, sentence structure, grammar, and usage.

Follow these steps with as much individual variances as necessary based on your students' needs and the actual sentence you selected for sentence cross-examination:

1. Choose a sentence from the target reading.
2. Present the sentence on chart paper, sentence strips, whiteboard, or SmartBoard.
3. Facilitate an in-depth discussion of what the sentence means and how the author expresses his or her idea by first inviting student input into meaning making.
4. Ask guiding questions—about the *who*, *what*, *when*, and *where* of the sentence.
5. Move onto discussing the *how* and *why* of the sentence, especially focusing on how and why the writer used certain words, phrases, language conventions, or grammar structures.
6. Use color-coding or other visually engaging methods to chunk the sentence into clauses or phrases.
7. Make note of one or more unique linguistic features of the sentence (active versus passive voice, relative clauses, heavy noun phrases, present or past participles, and so on) to call students' attention to select language complexities.
8. Utilize think-alouds as you pinpoint grammatical or stylistic choices in some (but not all of the) language chunks to keep the activity brief and engaging.
9. Invite students to use the sentence as mentor text and to create similar sentences of their own to practice internalizing the linguistic complexity represented in each sentence. Encourage them to select their own favorites as mentor texts to include when they are writing.

See Figure 3.9 for an example of how to conduct a sentence cross-examination with guiding questions in a social studies class using the following complex sentence:

> The northern states
> were undergoing rapid industrialization,
> which depended on wage labor,
> and while northerners disagreed among themselves about slavery,
> most believed
> it represented a direct challenge to their own rights and freedoms.

The sentence "The northern states were undergoing rapid industrialization, which depended on wage labor, and while northerners disagreed among themselves about slavery, most believed it represented a direct challenge to their own rights and freedoms" (Haskins 1998, 2) seems to be an ideal sentence for cross-examination. Although the actual meaning of each clause is relatively easy to comprehend, the sentence is composed of a complex grammatical structure that can be discussed and analyzed.

Figure 3.9 Cross-Examination Example Based on an Excerpt from *Black, Blue and Gray: African Americans in the Civil War* (Haskins 1998)

Guiding Questions for Meaning	Guiding Questions for Form and Usage
• Who is the sentence about? • What did the northern states experience? • What was the role of wage labor? • What did the northerners disagree about? • What did slavery represent for most northerners?	• The author uses the relative pronoun *which*. Find the noun phrase this pronoun refers to. (*Answer:* The pronoun refers to *rapid industrialization*.) • In the last segment of the sentence, the author refers to previously identified entities in a very concise way, such as *most* and *it*. How do we know who the author is talking about? (*Answer: Most* refers to the northerners and *it* refers to slavery. The previous sentence segment, "while northerners disagreed among themselves about slavery," identifies these two concepts clearly.) • Why does the author use the past continuous verb form *were undergoing* in this sentence? (*Answer:* It shows that the process took place gradually.)

Text-Level

Text-level work takes into account the way in which sentences are organized to create cohesive paragraphs and longer texts. To conduct text-level analysis of academic language, follow these guidelines:

Use a four-step approach and a practical tool such as a graphic organizer we adapted from Gottlieb (2011). (See Figure 3.10 for a completed text analysis grid on a science article discussed in a seventh-grade class.) Have students identify the overall purpose of the text; highlight the key words and phrases that give the main idea of the selection or are essential for understanding the authors' message; focus on a few, select sentence-level grammatical features such as verb tense, active or passive voice; and finally, examine the overall characteristics of the text with special attention to transitional words or other linguistic markers that help identify the text type or genre.

Talk-About

Supporting academic language development across the disciplines at the word, sentence, and text levels should not be perceived as teaching isolated skills; instead, consider the impact that academic conversations can have when students are engaged in discussion about the target content while using robust vocabulary, complex sentence structures, their own questioning, and appropriate transitions.

Enjoying any opportunity to talk with peers, your students will look forward to the moment when you ask them to get into groups for a Talk-About. Combining the best features of academic conversations (Zwiers and Crawford 2011) and Accountable Talk (Michaels et al. 2010), the Talk-About sets up a framework for using academic language in a small-group setting to help

Figure 3.10 Text Analysis Grid Based on *Journey to the Bottom of the Sea*

The Overall Purpose	**Key Words and Phrases**
This article reports on the experiences of the author when she went to the bottom of the Pacific Ocean in a submersible.	Pacific seafloor Ecosystems monthlong expedition microbe-collecting instrument
Grammatical Forms	**Genre or Text Type**

Great adjectives to describe what the author saw:
    blacker than black
    mile-and-a-half journey
    a towering mineral chimney
    revamped robotic arms
    efficient new LED lights
    glittering black rock of the seafloor
    scorching-hot black fluid
	First-person account of scientific exploration

Based on http://scienceworld.scholastic.com/Physics-News/2015/03/journey-to-the-bottom-of-the-sea

your students make sense of information and retain it. Instructional conversations (Goldenberg 1992; Tharp and Gallimore 1991) and other structured academic interaction frameworks have been researched for over three decades. More recently, Kate Kinsella's work (2012) on structured academic discourse and the Intentional Interaction Model discussed by Nicole Marie Sanchez and Lynn Darene Harper (2012) recognize the learner as an autonomous thinker who is actively engaged in the learning process along with his or her teacher. As Tharp and Gallimore (1991) observed, when teaching occurs through conversation, a classroom is transformed into a "community of learners" (5).

By no means is this type of conversation a student free-for-all. It follows very specific protocols that are established and reviewed by you and your class before anyone begins using them independently. Hakuta and colleagues (2013) suggest what they call the *Conversation Analysis Tool* to analyze student-to-student conversations. The two dimensions they focus on are:

- turns that build *on* other students' turns to *build up* an idea
- turns that focus on the *knowledge or skills* of the lesson's learning objectives (or Learning Targets).

These authors look for evidence of students prompting others and describing thinking, language, or content understandings that are part of a lesson. Their goal for students is that they effectively build up a cogent and complete idea and that they use the lesson's language or content understandings to do so.

More recently, Zwiers, O'Hara, and Pritchard (2014) present their *Constructive Conversation Skills Poster* that identifies multiple ways that students can build an idea. They suggest that students initiate their own questions, ask questions to clarify something that has been said, fortify the conversation by asking for examples and evidence, and negotiate differences of opinion.

Before releasing students to engage in a Talk-About (or a small-group academic conversation) of their own, read a short text together and model for them the types of questions and responses that promote such a conversation. Co-construct an anchor chart of the questions and sentence starters that your students come up with and place it on your wall for future independent student conversations. You might also provide them with a Talk-About Sentence Starters Foldable (see Figure 3.11) that offers additional scaffolding for their conversations and keeps students more fully engaged.

Figure 3.11 My Talk-About Sentence Starters Foldable to Scaffold Academic Conversations

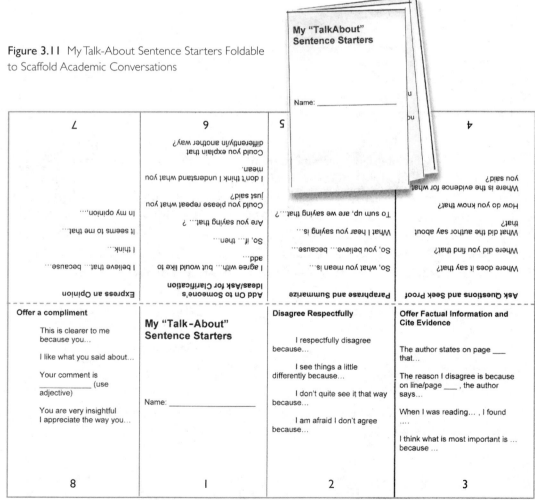

When students are ready to try these conversations without your guidance (to talk about, e.g., the pros and cons of different types of governments, the comparison of life in different ecosystems, how a writer engages a reader's interest, which type of music is most soothing and what elements it contains), select a group of five or six students you think will be able to handle this routine's protocols and have them create an inner circle. As the rest of the class looks on, encourage these students to conduct the academic conversation on their own. Ask the outer circle to list what types of interactions they observe. You can give them a checklist to tally these interactions.

Once you feel that students are confident enough to try this routine on their own, place them into heterogeneous groups of four to five members. Then, follow these steps:

1. Remind students that the goal of this group conversation is to promote *a dialogue where all students are involved.*

2. Tell them they will be evaluating their own participation, as well as their group's ability to collaborate, after the Talk-About is over. To develop shared student responsibility for this routine, have them evaluate their group by completing a checklist. See Figure 3.12 for a checklist of behaviors for students to focus on when engaged in a Talk-About.

3. If needed, provide students with a note-taking page that you developed in advance. The page might include written questions that will guide the conversation. It might include a graphic organizer or a page with sections and boxes for recording what each student learns from his or her conversation with peers. The handout can be blank, or you can partially fill it in to scaffold students who might benefit from some notes.

4. Keep the conversations short at first (no more than five to ten minutes) until students become comfortable with this routine. Rotate among the groups, refocusing learners and modeling good conversational skills.

5. After the set amount of time, regroup as a whole class and share out main ideas and details about the topic. (During this time you will be able to check for accuracy and address any misconceptions students may have.)

As educators, you know that "the person talking is probably thinking" (Fisher and Frey 2014a, 18). Or, as David Sousa (2011a) so aptly put it, "Whoever explains learns" (101). Keep these quotes in mind as you make plans for your students to initiate, build, and evaluate their independent conversations. The less we talk and the more students speak, the greater likelihood our learners will be engaged in critical thinking that increases comprehension (Murphy et al. 2009).

All content teachers need to teach academic English as well as the language of their disciplines. Finding the time to incorporate literacy instruction into content lessons will be a challenge. Yet, we urge you to find ways to implement language and literacy routines in all of your classes so students become proficient at initiating and participating in a range of collaborative discussions with diverse partners.

Figure 3.12 Talk-About Self-Evaluation Checklist

Check	Questions for Self-Evaluation	Reflections on My Participation
☐	Did I offer a compliment to a group member?	
☐	Did I disagree respectfully?	
☐	Did I offer factual information and cite evidence?	
☐	Did I paraphrase or summarize?	
☐	Did I initiate questions?	
☐	Did I ask questions to seek proof?	
☐	Did I add on to someone else's ideas or ask for clarification?	
☐	Did I fortify the conversation by asking for examples?	
☐	Did I offer an opinion or make a counterclaim?	

What should I focus on during my next conversation?

1.

2.

3.

HOMEWORK ROUTINES

Homework can be a challenge for secondary students. They often juggle academic demands with after-school activities and responsibilities. For this reason, we suggest some engaging variations on the homework theme.

Choice Homework Night

To spice up your homework regimen and increase the number of students who actually take the time to do it, we suggest a routine that has worked well in countless classrooms. Rather than just assigning students questions to be answered after a reading assignment or problems to practice after a math lesson, present students with a few homework *options*. See Figure 3.13 for examples of math Choice Homework. We have included tiered choices that provide practice at the grade level or provide challenge at an advanced level. Some considerations when designing this routine for your classroom:

- All options should be modeled before you add them to the list.
- Choice Homework should be given only once a week.
- Choice Homework is not to be graded. The purpose of giving choices is to generate enthusiasm for your discipline.
- Have students share out in small groups. Visit all groups and simply check for completion of one of the options.
- If you feel you must give a grade, keep it simple with a check (✔), check plus (✔+), or a zero (0) for not completing the task.
- Given on a Monday and due on Friday, or given on a Thursday and due on Monday, the Choice Homework routine is more sustainable for students.

Figure 3.13 Examples of Tiered Choice Homework for Math Class

On-grade-level choices

- IM a note to a friend who missed today's lesson. Be sure to include vocabulary, examples, key understandings, etc. Print out the note.
- Choose two math problems from tonight's assignment. Explain in words how to solve them. Be sure to include the language of math, vocabulary, examples, key understandings, tips, and hints.
- Create a visual describing today's concept. Introduce the topic and provide specific steps (using math language) for solving it. Offer tips and hints to keep in mind.

Challenge choices

- Create one page for our student-generated classroom math textbook on today's concept. Include model problems with highlighted sections (and corresponding explanations); use the "language of math"; provide tips/hints; suggest an online game or practice activity by providing the URL.
- Respond on the class Google Doc to challenging questions that include solving problems that require working backward, creating original word problems with answers, or answering "what if" questions ("What if we double the radius; what impact will it have on the area?").
- Create a one- to two-minute teaching video or podcast that teaches today's concept for placement on our classroom website. (You can use the Educreations App for this choice.)

Foldable

Providing students with the opportunity to create a Foldable for homework once or twice a unit is a creative way of having students reflect on the *big ideas*. This hands-on, minds-on approach to homework is sure to attract high levels of engagement. According to the foremost authority on the subject of Foldables, Dinah Zike, "Foldables are three-dimensional graphic organizers that take complicated data and information and make it visual and kinesthetic." (See her website for more information and examples: www.dinah.com/faq/faq.php.) By folding paper in almost infinite ways, you can create graphic organizers (essentially, three-dimensional charts or matrices) that help students organize ideas and retain them better. One of the simplest and most useful ways to fold the paper is as a three-tab Foldable.

Although it's tempting to use the Foldable just for low-level recall with illustrations and vocabulary, at the secondary level it is more rigorous when used to show relationships, both linguistically and nonlinguistically, as well as critical thinking: cause and effect, comparison and contrast, sequence, change over time, and so on. By adding an essential question along the bottom of the Foldable (start by gently folding an 8½-by-11-inch paper in half vertically, and then creasing it after leaving a half-inch for writing the question along the bottom), you can raise the complexity of this visual and kinesthetic activity. You can level the questions for different groups of students, thereby differentiating this routine further. See Figures 3.14, 3.15, and 3.16 for examples of Foldables designed by a high school English teacher for different grade-level classes.

Teacher-2-Teacher

In our cotaught English class, we use the Foldable as an alternative to paragraph writing. When we tell the kids, "We're going to be writing today," they cringe. However, when we tell them we are going to be creating a Foldable today, they have a much better attitude. They can handle exploring Shakespeare's use of light and dark imagery. When we tell them to look for two pieces of textual evidence that explore light and dark imagery, they can find that. When we tell them to analyze each piece of textual evidence, they can complete that. When we tell them to create a claim based on the textual evidence, they can do that.

The Foldable requires students to put together all the pieces that they would need for a well-developed paragraph, but they do not see this task that way. They arrive at their own understanding of the text in a sophisticated manner, while not feeling the prescribed dread associated with "writing today."

Foldables can be graded as the sole writing assignment or turned into a planning page or prewriting activity for a formal paragraph or essay.

Brittany Baran, teacher of high school English, South Huntington School District

Figure 3.14 Front, Inside, and Back of a Ninth-Grader's Foldable Comparing Two Informational Texts

Text #5: Kids Need Structure
Author: Colin Powell
Year Published: 2012

Text #6: Dr. Montessori's Own Handbook
Author: Maria Montessori
Year Published: 1914

How do the educational methods of Powell and Montessori differ?

Claim: Powell believes that structure in education ~~will~~ is the best method for success in students.
• "A child who has not been read to is in danger when that child gets to school." (Lines 55-56).
• "...the kids who didn't have structure and minding in the beginning start to realize they're behind, and what do they do? They act it out." (Lines 70-72).
• "If you're not at the right reading level at third grade, you are a candidate for jail at age 18..." (Lines 73-74).

Claim: Montessori believes that ~~teachers~~ should give students freedom and they shouldn't intervene with learning.
• "It is necessary for the teacher to guide the child without letting him feel her presence too much...never be the obstacle between the child and his experience." (Lines 2-5).
• "Then we shall notice that...he has initiative, he chooses his own work, persists in it." (Lines 11-12).
• "Let us leave the life free to develop within the limits of the good, and let us observe this inner life developing" (Lines 47-49).

How do the educational methods of Powell and Montessori differ?

I think that Maria Montessori's method of education is better. With her method, students will enjoy learning and will search for their own learning. In Powell's method, students will only learn what they are forced to and they will resent their teacher for most of their education.

10/10
Very nicely done!

Max

Figure 3.15 Front and Inside of a Ninth-Grader's Foldable Exploring Shakespeare's Use of Light and Dark Imagery in *Romeo and Juliet*

continues

Textual Evidence:

"Yond light is not day light; I know it, I. It is meteor that the Sun exhales. To be to thee this night a torch bearer and light thee on thy way to mantua, Therefore stay yet; thou needst not to be gone"

(SHAKESPEARE 157 lines 12-16)

Analysis:
Juliet is trying to keep Romeo from leaving because once daylight comes he has to leave

Textual Evidence:

"Some say the lark makes sweet divisons; This doth not so, for she divideth us"

(SHAKESPEARE 157 lines 29-30)

Analysis:
She's talking about how the morning birds, the larks are upsetting to her because once they play their song her love Romeo has to leave.

Their relationship is a light that can only be kept in the Dark. because in light they will be seperated

Figure 3.16 Front and Inside of an Eleventh-Grader's Foldable Exploring Themes in *Catcher in the Rye*

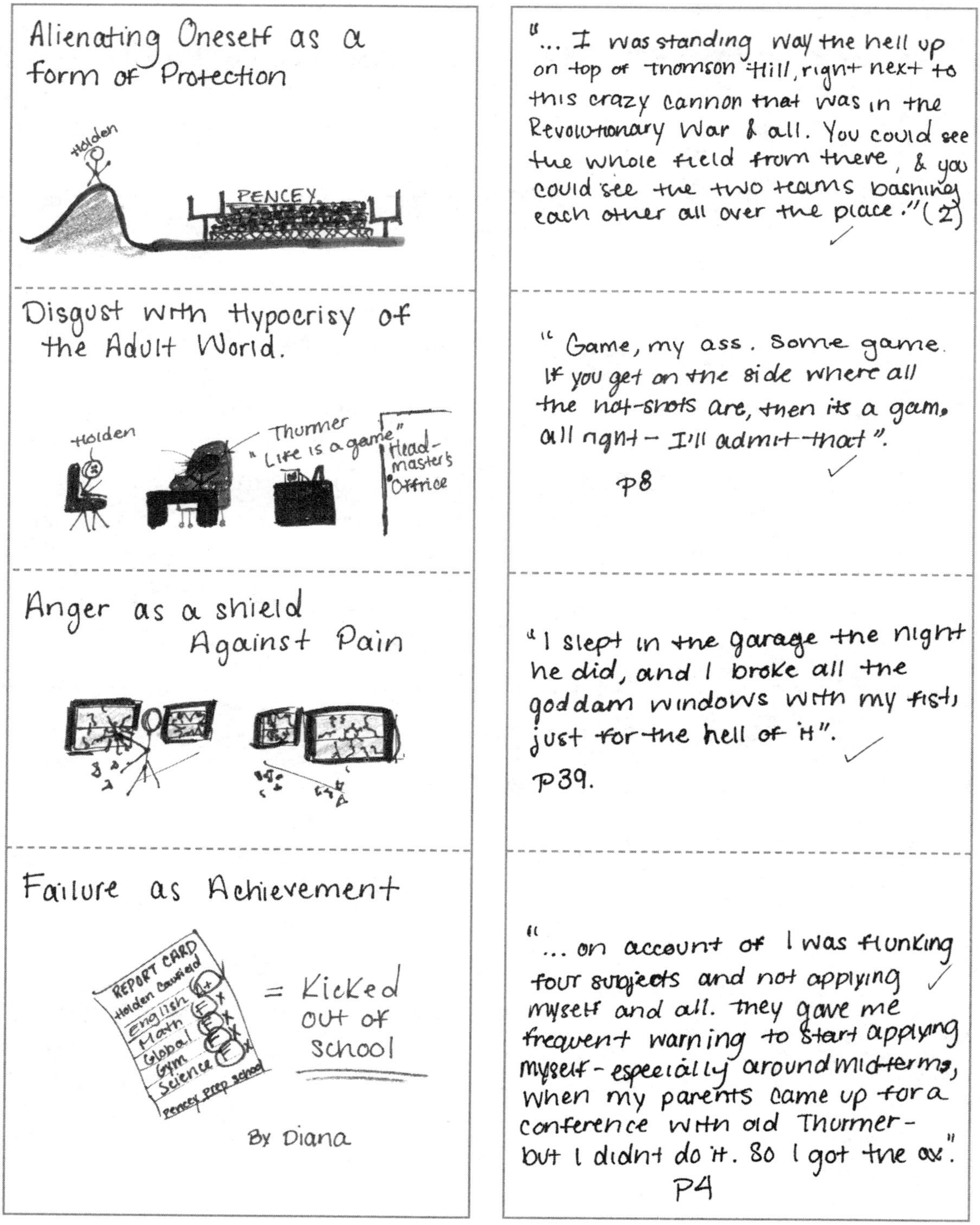

Alienating Oneself as a form of Protection

Holden

PENCEY

"... I was standing way the hell up on top of Thomson Hill, right next to this crazy cannon that was in the Revolutionary War & all. You could see the whole field from there, & you could see the two teams bashing each other all over the place." (2)

Disgust with Hypocrisy of the Adult World.

Holden
Thurmer
"Life is a game"
Head-master's Office

" Game, my ass. Some game. If you get on the side where all the hot-shots are, then its a game, all right – I'll admit that".
P8

Anger as a shield Against Pain

"I slept in the garage the night he did, and I broke all the goddam windows with my fist, just for the hell of it".
P39.

Failure as Achievement

REPORT CARD
Holden Caurield
English
Math
Global
Gym
Science
Pencey Prep School

= Kicked out of school

By Diana

"... on account of I was flunking four subjects and not applying myself and all. They gave me frequent warning to start applying myself – especially around midterms, when my parents came up for a conference with old Thurmer – but I didn't do it. So I got the ax."
P4

ROUTINE 3 **End-of-Unit Routines**

At the end of each unit, we recommend you let students synthesize their learning through a choice of routines. Although you may still use a pen-and-pencil test as a summative assessment, we encourage you to provide additional opportunities for students to engage in collaborative reviews, discussions, and presentations.

Recognizing that tests are not the only way to assess learners, numerous teachers we work with try to integrate an *alternative assessment* routine for each or, at least, every other unit. Sometimes, these alternatives take the form of protracted project-based learning activities, but more often, because of time constraints at the secondary level, the alternative may simply be a list or menu of different ways that students may choose to respond to the curriculum.

COLLABORATIVE REVIEW ROUTINES

We learn as we put our thoughts into words and speak them. This simple act is quite complex, as it helps us to conceptualize, organize ideas, solve problems, and explain ourselves to others and be understood. As your students use the following collaborative routines and put their ideas into words, they will be able to take more responsibility for their own learning, as you facilitate from the sidelines. "All learning floats on a sea of talk," psycholinguist James Britton (1970, 164) apprises us. For this very reason, we offer you several choices for having students learn by collaborating.

Alphabet Round-Up

One routine for winding up a unit is the alphabet roundup, adapted from Buehl's (2001) sequential roundtable alphabet. We want students to synthesize their newly learned vocabulary and new understandings and to be able fluently communicate these ideas. The alphabet roundup is a constructive way to build this fluency. (See the companion resources, at heinemann.com/products/E07434.aspx, for a template you can use.)

Be sure to leave enough room in each box of the alphabet grid so that students can write *several* terms or phrases that begin with each letter, as they reflect on the topic. Group students into teams of four and give every student a grid. Time students *for one minute* while each member notes on his or her grid as many connections (words or phrases) as come to mind. Then, have the students pass their grids clockwise. Encourage students *not to write the same* word(s) or phrase(s) on the next grid passed to them but, rather, encourage them to read their peers' words and phrases and think of new connections. Reading what other group members have recorded will help spark additional memories and associations. Continue this way until all group members have had a chance to record on *each* of their team members' grids.

Then, give each team five minutes to openly discuss the topic using the recorded language and to respond to the essential question that you pose (What makes a civilization great? How do effective writers hook and retain their readers' attention? How do destructive weather events impact a society? Which nutrients and in what amounts should we consume daily? What is the future of energy in the United States? Which is the best strategy for problem solving?) One of the best ways to learn vocabulary is by using it. This vocabulary/concept summary routine allows students to think about words, to use them in academic conversations, and then to reorganize the words into meaningful written responses to essential questions (the questions that you posed at the beginning of the unit). See Figures 3.17 and 3.18 for examples of Alphabet Round-ups.

COACH'S NOTES

If you have a group of English language learners with emerging language, you can allow these students to write a summary, rather than an argument, using the vocabulary. Or, you could guide them with questions or provide them with sentence starters to scaffold their writing.

Figure 3.17 An Alphabet Roundup About World War II Completed by a High School Social Studies Student

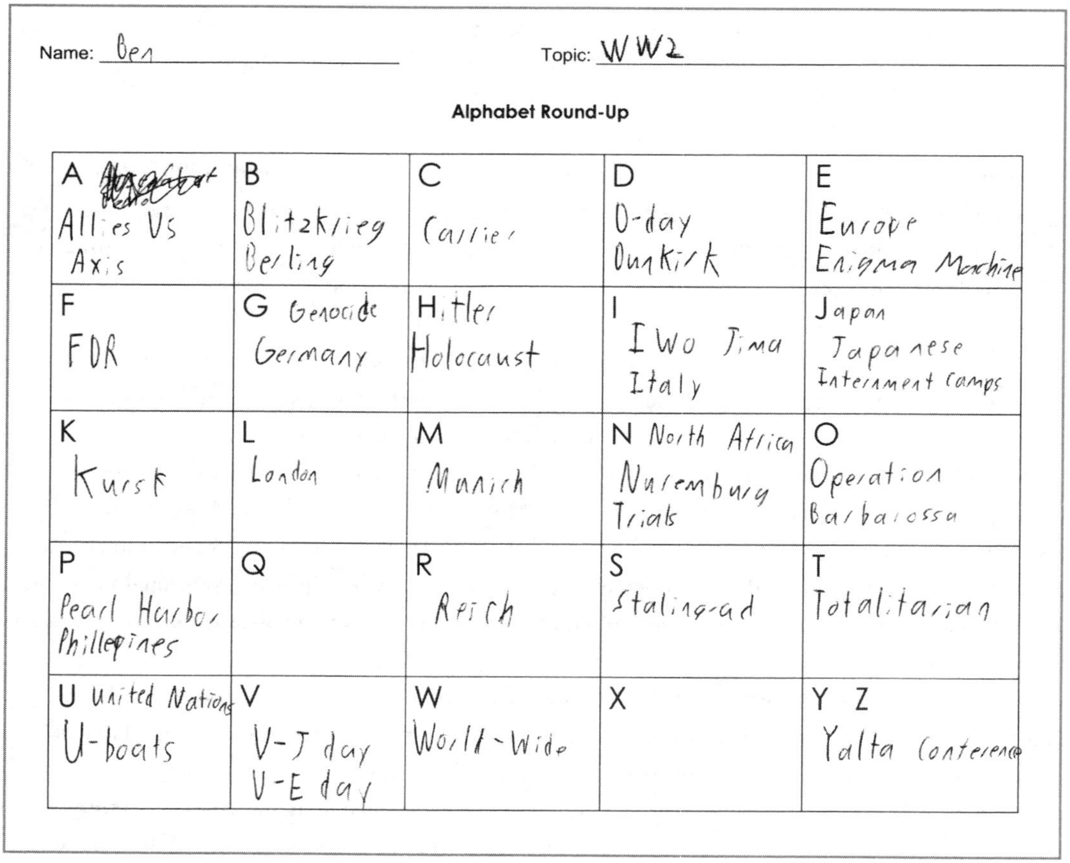

Name: Ben   Topic: WW2

Alphabet Round-Up

A	B	C	D	E
Allies Vs Axis	Blitzkrieg Berling	Carrier	D-day Dunkirk	Europe Enigma Machine
F FDR	G Genocide Germany	Hitler Holocaust	I Iwo Jima Italy	Japan Japanese Internment Camps
K Kursk	L London	M Munich	N North Africa Nuremburg Trials	O Operation Barbarossa
P Pearl Harbor Phillepines	Q	R Reich	S Stalingrad	T Totalitarian
U United Nations U-boats	V V-J day V-E day	W World-Wide	X	Y Z Yalta Conference

Figure 3.18 An Alphabet Roundup on a Science Topic by an Eighth-Grade Student

Name: Zach			**Topic:** Weather	

Alphabet Round-Up

Atmosphereic Preassure	Barrometric Preassure	Cold Front	Dew Point	Evaporation
Fahrenheit	Global Warming	Hurricaine	Inches of mercury	Jet Stream
Kelvin	Latitude	Millibar	Noreaster	Occluded front
Precipitation	Quake	Rain	Station model	Transvaporation
Umbrella	Visiblity	Warm Front	X	Y Z

ThinkTank

Used at the end of a unit, instead of as a during-class routine as described in Chapter 2, the Think-Tank is a short collaborative activity that will provide five minutes of speaking and listening for all students. Ask students to list key ideas or illustrate their understanding of a particular concept, to answer one of the unit's essential questions, to solve a particular type of problem, or to note a sequence of events or steps.

Be sure to use the ThinkTank charts, with their rich vocabulary and content information, for a follow-up writing activity. You can ask your students to use the recorded details to write a summary of the topic; to compose an argument while citing evidence provided on the charts; to compare two different ideas, places, stories, or characters; or to create an informative or explanatory text (perhaps, a study guide) from the notes on the ThinkTanks. The ThinkTanks can even be "tiered," or leveled, by providing groups with *different* questions or ways to respond, rather than giving each group the same task. See Figure 3.19 where a math high school teacher engages each of her algebra students in a tiered ThinkTank with a "just-right" challenge.

As educators, it is our job to teach children with a variety of abilities and learning styles to reach their maximum potential. This can be a difficult task at times. During our Inclusion Common Core Algebra 1 Class, we tiered a concluding activity by using the math ThinkTank. Each group was formed according to students' abilities. The groups had to brainstorm about the parent function they were assigned. Each group had success (within their ability level), by exchanging ideas while participating in a fun activity! Their success led to positive attitudes that were evident during subsequent math classes.

Ramona Woods and Jennifer Forrester,
high school math teachers

Figure 3.19 ThinkTank Discussion in Algebra

Stations

As a collaborative activity, the stations routine ranks high in student popularity. Most of the teachers we have worked with choose to use the stations routine at the end of a unit to make reviewing a more dynamic and meaningful process than the usual review sheet method. Stations liven up your classroom, maximize engagement, and increase opportunities for collaboration and review.

Students rotate through a set of teacher-designed stations with engaging names (e.g., the quotation station, the manipulation station, the visualization station, etc.) and complete essential tasks related to the unit. See the "Coach's Notes" section in this chapter for ideas for other stations. Although high school students might complain about the movement that the routine requires, most middle school students will welcome the opportunity to move around and talk with their peers. Funnel their energy into this routine. With reluctant high school students who prefer to stay in their seats, you can change the routine so that all students remain sitting with one group and the task rotates from group to group. Teachers enjoy the flexibility of working with students who need additional attention; as small groups busily move through a set of short activities, they can attend to these learners.

- **For social studies: Set up stations for students to practice analyzing authentic documents. Rotating through multiple stations, groups will look at the document (chart, graph, map, photo, political cartoon, etc.) they find at each station, discuss what conclusions they draw (perhaps guided by teacher-prepared questions), and, individually, record notes.**

- **For math:** Michelle Rand, middle school math teacher, says, "I used stations to help students with fluency of converting fractions, decimals, and percents. Each station represented a different conversion. In addition to these stations, I always run a teacher station where I provide small-group instruction for learners at all levels."
- **For English language arts:** Have students take the first draft of an individual piece of writing and move through five editing stations. At each station, they might find an example of a particular writing craft or skill to include in their own piece of writing.

You may have noticed that many of our recommended routines incorporate several literacy skills at once. You might decide to develop a set of stations that involve less speaking and listening and more reading and writing. The possibilities for creating stations are endless.

COACH'S NOTES

Use the following stations to have your students engage with their texts, labs, writing, and/or content:

- *Observation/identification station:* Students observe, identify, describe, analyze, sort, categorize.
- *Justification station:* Students tell why something occurs, cite evidence, support with details, persuade others.
- *Documentation station:* Students analyze and interpret primary source documents, charts, graphs, maps, speeches.
- *Evaluation station:* Students judge the actions of others, prioritize the needs, evaluate the effectiveness of a particular document or policy.

Follow these steps to implement a set of stations at the end of your unit:

1. Label folded index cards with numbers (1, 2, 3, 4, etc.) to identify your stations.
2. At each station (several desks grouped together, a table, a few desks placed just outside your door, etc.), place a task card that contains written instructions for what students must do at the station.
3. Design the task for each station to take about the same amount of time. Some teachers include an early finisher's activity (a bonus or challenge question, a creative task, an extension activity, or an assessment question that will be assigned for homework) that students can work on for a minute or two if they complete a station before time is up.

4. Indicate when it's time to move to the next station by using a chime, a bell, a light, or some other agreed-upon signal.

5. Make sure that each student has his or her own clipboard, Foldable, graphic organizer, or notebook to record information.

6. Encourage the group members to discuss the task or question together and share their ideas out loud.

7. Although the conversation is collaborative, the resulting finished product is completed individually. Each student must complete his or her own responses in writing or drawing.

Some teachers organize a set of stations over the course of a week, having students visit one station a day. Other teachers prefer to design short tasks (from five to eight minutes) and have students complete them all in one or two days. Most teachers plan activities that last anywhere from five to fifteen minutes. The shorter the activities, the more frequently you will use the stations routine.

Each time students engage in this routine, they will transition more smoothly from station to station and they will focus more quickly on the task at hand. See the anchor chart about GROUPs in Figure 3.20 that Michelle Rand displays in her classroom to remind students of behaviors that they should display while collaborating. This routine is an excellent way for students to talk about what they have learned in a unit or to practice a skill by discussing or doing it with someone else. As they talk, they learn.

Figure 3.20 GROUP Work Expectations

Text Talk

Text Talk involves individual student reflection followed by collaboration. Providing another opportunity for students to communicate their ideas about a chosen text, this routine is eagerly carried out by students because they get to talk with their peers. Read how one teacher integrates this comprehension routine in her class of English language learners.

Teacher-2-Teacher

After a whole-class discussion, I sometimes turn to a Text Talk activity to check for comprehension. (See Figure 3.21 where students wrote silently and Figure 3.22 for a completed Text Talk chart.) Sitting in small groups, students receive one sheet of chart paper and a question about the passage or section of a novel that we've been reading and discussing. All communication at this point is through writing; students may not speak to one another as they respond on the chart. After five to ten minutes, they are ready and eager to discuss their ideas. My students love to do this!

Hilcia Brandt, middle school English as a second language teacher

Figure 3.21 Students Write Silently—The First Step in a Text Talk

Figure 3.22 One Group's Completed Text Talk Chart

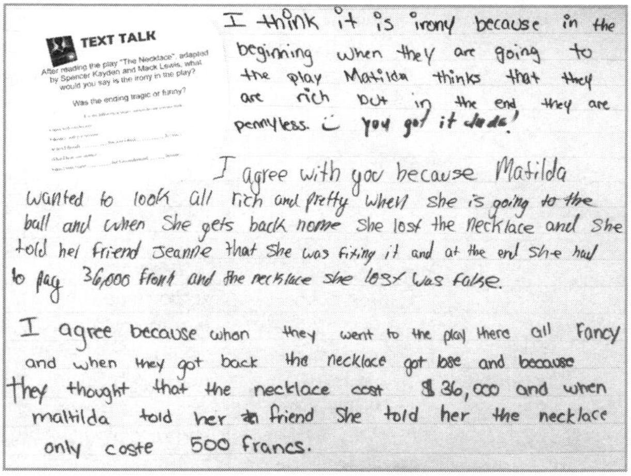

MathChat!

Similar to Socratic circles, academic conversations, Accountable Talk, and the Talk-About routines previously discussed, MathChat! invites learners to speak and collaborate about math problem solving (see Figure 3.23 where students run their own MathChat! discussion). Discussing homework problems or processing mathematical understandings from the day's lesson or a completed unit, an inner circle of four to six students takes the role of problem solvers as they engage in the following:

- collaborative *discussion*
- *analysis* of the problem
- presenting *main ideas*
- elaborating on the *necessary steps* to take
- *providing tips or hints* for solving this type of problem
- *asking questions* to clarify peer responses

Figure 3.23 Student-Directed MathChat! Discussion Rubric

Name: _____ Class: _____ Date: _____

	4 Advanced	3 Proficient	2 Emerging	1 Beginning	0 Off Task	Score
Using Accountable Talk	Whole-class discussion was led by the scholars with little teacher assistance. Scholars built on each other's remarks and used accountable talk stems at all times to create a positive, productive discussion. Student discussion reflects multiple perspectives and deep content knowledge.	Whole-class discussion is led by scholars with some teacher assistance. Scholars build on and respond respectfully to other scholars' remarks to create a fluid conversation. While using accountable stems, scholars showed evidence of content knowledge.	Discussion is led by scholars with some teacher assistance. Conversation lacks depth, expresses views/restates questions or points that were previously made.	Discussion is addressed at the teacher, not to each other and does not clearly use accountable talk stems to express ideas. Students do not listen actively to one another in order to have a productive conversation.	Students were unwilling or unprepared to refer to text evidence or to share their ideas in a discussion.	
Asking Questions and Solving Problems Did every scholar participate?	Actively incorporates every student into the discussion by summarizing, building on, clarifying, verifying, or challenging ideas or conclusions. Qualifies or justifies own views and understanding and makes new connections from the evidence.	Incorporates some students into the discussion by summarizing, building on, clarifying, verifying, or challenging ideas or conclusions and making new connections from the evidence and reasoning presented.	Incorporates only a few students into the discussion by summarizing, building on, clarifying, verifying, or challenging ideas or conclusions.	Does not incorporate others into the discussion or qualify/justify own views and understanding.	Disrespectful of others. Behavior indicates total and absolute non-involvement with group or discussion.	
Communication	Always uses sources and mathematical evidence to support their claims and brings conversation to a deeper level.	Frequently uses sources and mathematical evidence to support their claims, but does not push others to deeper levels of thinking.	Occasionally uses sound logical reasoning or examples to support their opinions and claims.	Does not use any sources, reasoning, or mathematical evidence to support their opinions, simply states their thoughts.	No productive ideas or use of resources or mathematical evidence.	

Developed by Rich Roder, Michelle Rand, Daniel Page, and Christina Vagenas, Queens United Middle School. Adapted with permission.

- *fortifying the conversation* by adding further explanation
- *using discipline-specific words* from a word list in their notebook
- *using academic language* from a classroom word wall.

For five to eight minutes, the inner circle takes part in this routine, as the rest of the class actively engages in one outer-circle task such as:

- *tallying how many times* each member of the inner group uses discipline-specific vocabulary and refers to mathematical content and concepts
- *tallying how many times* each member of the inner group uses academic language
- *noting the best tips and hints suggested* for solving this type of problem
- *listing on the board* two or three of the most important points raised
- *using a check-off list,* noting each time someone makes a connection:
  - compares to something else ("This is like . . ." "This is different from . . .")
  - notes a sequence ("First, . . . next, . . . then, . . .", etc.)
  - offers an additional strategy to solve the same problem ("You can also solve this by . . ." "Another way of doing this is . . .")
  - fortifies the conversation ("I'd like to add . . ." "In addition, . . .")
  - clarifies a peer's response ("What he means is . . .").

Rich Roder, the principal of Queens United Middle School, and three of his teachers adapted their school-wide discussion rubric to align with the MathChat! routine. You can also find it on the companion website, at heinemann.com/products/E07434.aspx, and use it to evaluate the participants in your own classes.

Special Considerations

You may have to adapt some of the routines described in this chapter to better suit your unique situation. Among other considerations, the size of your classroom, numbers of students, length of the period, and the availability of technology might necessitate tweaking some of the routines to make them more efficient and useable.

What if you teach over 100 students each day?

Having large numbers of students can make it more difficult for you to work with certain routines. There are more students to get to know and different needs to meet. There is more homework to grade. How will you attend to these and other obstacles to classroom management?

A unique challenge that you may face in addition to having many students on your roster might be overcrowded classrooms. One of the ways you can address this concern is not to have students move around in your filled-to-capacity room. Keep students in their seats and *rotate the task* to each group in a box or folder. This way, the routine will flow better as there will be fewer disturbances caused by congested pathways. Another way to address large numbers of students is to shorten the routine, so that the task does not take as long. Additionally, you can choose to use an inner- and outer-circle format that is easier to manage for the Talk-About, rather than trying to manage six or seven small groups that are working separately.

Assign students roles to help with checking assignments, passing out materials, and collecting papers and supplies. Work on strategies for getting to know your students because it will be harder to do so in large classes. Use class surveys or learning log journals for students to share their interests, their accomplishments, and their challenges. During a test day, comment in your students' journals. Rotate your focus on a different set of students every few days so no one falls through the cracks (Alber 2015). For the stations routine, you might create two groups of students that rotate through three tasks, rather than six groups of students rotating through six tasks. (See Figure 3.24 to envision this set-up.) Run in this way, the stations activity will take half the time.

Figure 3.24 Classroom Stations Flowchart

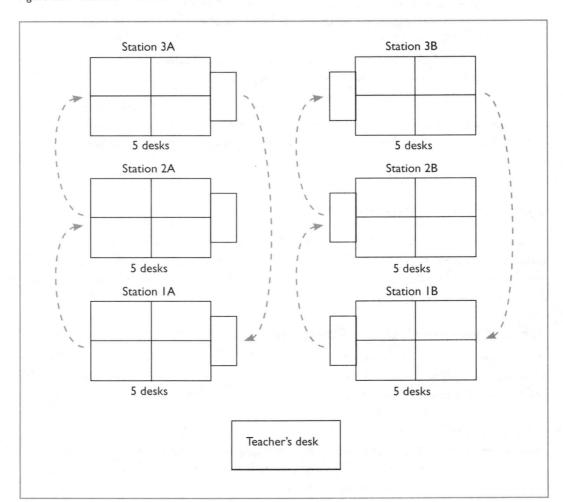

Finally, you should consider implementing Choice Homework Night at least once a week. This routine will energize your class while cutting down the time needed to grade homework.

What if you teach multiple courses each semester?

The best way to save preparation time for multiple courses is to create *generic* tasks, checklists, and assessments that can be used in any class.

What if you don't have your own classroom?

Not having your own classroom is always a problematic challenge for teachers. In this situation, unfortunately, you will probably use some of the routines where students move a bit less. You will need to post permanent numbers around the rooms you visit (after negotiating space needs with the teachers whose classrooms you use) so that you don't need any preparation time to break into Carousel Brainstorming or the ThinkTank routine. Most of the instructions for your routines will need to be written ahead of time and carried with you from class to class on your flash drive or in Dropbox.

What if your class period is longer than the typical forty- to forty-four minute class?

In this case, you will actually have more time to use the routines we suggest. Some of the routines (stations, making arguments, Carousel Brainstorming, and the Talk-About) will be more effective if you have additional time for students' engagement. When you plan your lessons, be sure to vary presentation of new material or prepared PowerPoint presentations with some of the speaking and collaborating routines recommended. This will ensure that you provide a balance of both teacher-directed and student-driven learning that can take place more often during longer classes.

What if you want to incorporate technology?

If you have access to laptops (or other mobile devices), you use Apps like Google Docs so that students can work together to answer questions or do research on the same document. Additionally, laptops can be used during the stations routine. By grouping two laptops together and creating one station, you can have four to six students rotate through this station, while using a minimum number of devices. Using mobile devices, the virtual exploration routine can become an opportunity for students to practice self-regulation rather than being led through a teacher-directed activity.

Teacher-2-Teacher

As more districts adopt one-to-one technology, teachers have the ability to transform the student writing experience. My students publish all of their writing, even summative written exams, publicly using a class blog. This provides an authentic audience for students; they no longer write solely for the teacher. Students quickly learn the routine of posting writing

A Final Thought

As you choose the routines you prefer for each unit, keep in mind that using them as frequently as possible will prepare your students to use them independently. We believe that high standards don't need to compete with joyous learning in the secondary classroom. By engaging your students in creative routines that hook and focus them at the beginning of a unit, keep them engaged and provide them some choice during the unit, and offer opportunities for working and talking with peers to synthesize their understanding at the end of the unit, your students will enjoy your class more than ever.

Essential Questions for Individual Reflection, Collegial Circles, and Group Discussions

- *Why is it important to plan for before-, middle-, and end-of-unit routines?*

- *Which three routines can you see trying in your classroom? Why did you choose these?*

- *Which routines will you embrace to operationalize David Sousa's (2011a) quote, "Whoever explains learns" (101)?*

- *What are some of the challenges you anticipate as you try to implement some of the routines?*

- *Are there any other routines you have used successfully and can share with your colleagues?*

Reading is the foundation of life, an activity that people who are engaged with the world do all the time.

Rafe Esquith, *Teach Like Your Hair Is on Fire*

Chapter 4

ROUTINES FOR EACH MARKING PERIOD

Overview

In this chapter, we

- summarize research support for the authentic, independent, project-based learning routines we present
- establish routines to be implemented once or several times in each marking period
- present examples, templates, resources, and classroom vignettes along with recommendations from coaches to support the implementation of routines teachers use in each marking period
- discuss special considerations for variations in teaching assignments (large number of students, multiple courses or multiple sections of the same course, varied lengths of class periods) and technology integration.

Routines for Each Marking Period at a Glance

ROUTINE 1 - - ➤ **Independent Reading Routines**

Getting Started with Independent Reading

Sustaining Independent Reading
- Individual Support for Reading
- Interactions with Others

Celebrating and Sharing Reading
- Sharing Individual Reading Accomplishments Through Projects
- Individual or Group Presentations

ROUTINE 2 - - ➤ **Student-Directed Learning Routines**

Anchor Projects

Mini–Research Projects

Project-Based Learning

Genius Hour or Innovation Day

SOLE

Games for Learning

ROUTINE 3 - - ➤ **Outside-the-Classroom Routines**

Service-Learning (Community Engagement)

Field Trips and Guest Speakers

Shared Family Learning Experiences

What Does the Research Say About Authentic, Student-Driven Learning Experiences?

Kathryn R. Wentzel and Allan Wigfield (2009) remind us how challenging and complex students' academic lives are. They engage in a variety of academic learning tasks and are expected to meet grade-level standards in a range of instructional content areas; at the same time, they need to learn the norms of the school community, establish new relationships with peers and teachers each year, follow classroom rules, and, in general, participate in all activities related to their schooling. "Central to understanding children's success at these activities is motivation, that is, the energy they bring to these tasks, the beliefs, values and goals that determine which tasks they pursue and their persistence in achieving them, and the standards they set to determine when a task has been accomplished" (Wentzel and Wigfield 2009, 1).

Motivation might be extrinsic in nature and result in students working toward rewards outside themselves (grades, awards, honor society memberships, a formal recognition of achievement, getting into a college, and so on); however, intrinsic motivation that is driven by students' deep-rooted interest in or passion for a topic as well as opportunities for creative expressions fosters more lasting learning. Maureen Price-Mitchell (2010) notes that high levels of engagement do not grow out of daily homework assignments. Based on her study on adolescents' civic participation, she concludes that "highly engaged adolescents overcome intellectual, interpersonal, and intrapersonal challenges as a result of civic involvement; benefit from adult scaffolding; and are personally transformed by demanding service experiences" (ii). Adolescent psychologists as well as practitioners working with this age group agree that students need authentic opportunities to develop autonomy, to learn from their mistakes, to engage in inquiry-based explorations, and to find and define their own directions while working on reaching meaningful goals. Schools that provide such learning opportunities nurture a much desired pattern of lifelong learning in adolescents.

Routines for Each Marking Period

In this chapter, we establish routines for authentic learning opportunities with clear academic and literacy purposes. Courtney Cazden (2001) reminds us that "classrooms are complex social systems" (54), with a range of purpose for interaction, often well-established speaking rights, cultural differences in communication, and a lot of other variances. Secondary schools may become highly competitive learning environments with complex curricula to master. Yet, all students need to find their authentic voices, participate in opportunities for real-life learning experiences so they could establish agency (a sense of purpose) and autonomy (a sense of identity) for themselves. Furthermore, if there is a commitment in the school to create a *culture of literacy* and a *literate school culture*, Wolsey, Lapp, and Fisher (2010) suggest that "all students are to act and believe that literacy is valued and valuable" (10).

Based on their research on high schoolers' out-of-school experiences with reading and writing, Elizabeth Birr Moje, Melanie Overby, Nicole Tysvaer, and Karen Morris (2008) debunk several myths surrounding adolescent literacy and identify what young people value in what they read:

They like to read books about people like them, and not only in terms of race, ethnicity, age, class, or gender (although these features are important). They also like to identify with characters who are resilient through struggles, people who are working through relationships, people trying to figure out who they are. They want to read books and write texts that offer them social capital in the form of information, ideas for self-improvement, models for identities, or ways to maintain existing relationships and build new ones. (25)

Our beliefs and professional practice are aligned with the research of Moje et al. (2008) and Wolsey at al. (2010); we, too, suggest that students read text (both fiction and nonfiction) driven by personal interest and by their genuine motivation to build social and academic capital as well as to expand their social network. First, we outline a framework for independent reading routines that keep students engaged while maintaining an academic focus.

In addition to the reading routines, we suggest routines for student explorations that are self-directed and autonomous and lead to nurturing a desire for lifelong learning. Finally, we recommend ways you can take learning beyond the walls of the classroom and present instructional routines that lead to opportunities for authentic interactions with the real world.

ROUTINE 1 Independent Reading Routines

In his highly acclaimed publication poignantly titled *Readicide: How Schools Are Killing Reading and What You Can Do About It,* Kelly Gallagher (2009) claims that we are killing the love of reading partially because secondary literacy instruction has been largely limited to standardized test preparation. This notion is especially troubling when "reading has more impact on students' achievement than any other activity in school" (Miller 2009, 52).

Establishing and maintaining an independent reading routine that is sustained, enjoyable, and meaningful should be a critical goal for each marking period. Secondary students also need to see adults as role models engaged in reading and meaning-making. We are inspired by Penny Kittle (2013), who shows us how to do just that in *Book Love:* She firmly believes that "rich and rewarding reading lives are within reach for all of our students" (1), and she describes how she has engaged her secondary students in such reading experiences. Teachers like Sarah Krajewski (see the following Teacher-2-Teacher) share their own reading lives with their students, which motivates them to become readers for life. Just like Penny and Sarah, you can keep track of your own and your students' reading lives.

Teacher-2-Teacher

There's a section of my whiteboard I call "What's Mrs. Krajewski Reading?" and I update it weekly with my current book(s), the amount of pages I read the week before, and other popular books that I have either read or heard great things about (see Figure 4.1). I do not read during the first ten minutes of class; instead, I confer with students, write down book titles and page numbers, and so on. I also encourage them to "quiz" me about the books pictured on my board not only to prove I am reading, but so students can add to their "to-read list." I also maintain a digital bookshelf under a tab with the same name on my website where students can click on each book I have read, am currently reading, or am planning to read: www.clevehill.wnyric.org/webpages/skrajewski/

Sarah Krajewski, English teacher, Cleveland Hill High School, Buffalo, New York

Figure 4.1 Sarah Krajewski's Whiteboard Display of Her Reading Selections

GETTING STARTED WITH INDEPENDENT READING

Although sustained silent reading (SSR) and Drop Everything and Read (DEAR) programs are hallmarks of the elementary classroom, students in secondary grades also need time to read independently. Some course content may lend itself better to this routine than others, but even if you are not an English teacher, students benefit from independent reading of literacy or discipline-specific, informational texts. The best time to start independent reading is at the beginning of the year. Be prepared to show (not just tell) your students how engaging and satisfying reading will be. You will need to appeal to your students' emotional, cognitive, and social selves. See how Amanda Lentino from Ramapo Schools establishes an independent reading routine for each marking period.

Teacher-2-Teacher

At the beginning of each marking period, I reserve a class period for a trip to the school library. Students meet with the librarian and preview some of the books that we have put aside. We chose the books based on a reading interest inventory students completed during the first week of school. Students browse the books, which are spread out on the tables and categorized by topics/subjects. Once students have an idea of what they would like to read, they can reserve the book and silently read somewhere in the library. If a student cannot find a book in the school library, we browse the Internet until we find one of interest.

When I introduce students to independent reading, they choose a project from a full list of options to complete by the end of the marking period. I also introduce the students to the six notice and note signposts (Beers and Probst 2012) and give them a bookmark with all six notice and note signs listed to keep in their independent reading books.

Every Friday is independent reading day. Students come into class and immediately begin reading. While students read, I walk around the room to monitor their reading, and I hold reading conferences with individual students in the back of the room. At the end of the class period, students submit at least one notice and note signpost chart utilizing Beers and Probst's work. During the last week of the marking period, students submit a project on their independent reading books and give a brief presentation to the class. (See Figures 4.2a and 4.2b for examples of completed projects.)

Amanda Lentino, teacher of English and journalism

Figures 4.2a and 4.2b Independent Reading Projects from Amanda Lentino's class

SUSTAINING INDEPENDENT READING

Students will also benefit from routines that help sustain the initiative and keep the excitement and momentum going. To sustain independent reading, consider offering your students both individual support in the form of guidance and mentoring, as well as group support that also serves as a vehicle for peer motivation. In addition, create an inviting space for independent reading, as Jessica Antonucci does in her eighth-grade English classroom (Figures 4.3a and 4.3b).

Figures 4.3a and 4.3b Eighth Graders Reading in a Comfortable Spot

Individual Support for Reading

If you choose to meet with your students individually, conference time must be set aside on a regular basis, at least once or twice a marking period. A conference about students' independent reading may take the form of an instructional conversation that helps students reflect on their own reading lives and helps you monitor students' reading choices, strategy use, and progression. Ask students to explain what they like to read, how much they read, how they make a selection, and what they are planning to read next.

We look to Penny Kittle (2013) for guidance on engaging adolescent readers in quarterly reading reflections. We adapted her framework and created a protocol for inviting students to participate in the reflection process. We invite you to follow a specific routine consisting of these five steps each marking period:

Step 1: Discuss Difficulty

Have students reflect on what makes a book difficult and what strategies they use to get through a challenging read. Invite them to monitor their growth in each marking period and reflect on how they improved tackling difficulties encountered while reading independently.

Step 2: Discuss Reading Rate

Have students keep track of how many pages they read each week. Have them see if there is a pattern to their stamina and reflect on what helps them keep reading and what slows them down.

Step 3: Discuss Favorite Books

Have students identify one or more favorite texts in each marking period and summarize them. These short written reports may be shared with other students or used in a portfolio.

Step 4: Discuss Goals

Invite students to set new goals for each marking period, considering both how much they are planning to read and what type of reading they will choose.

Step 5: Have Students Write a Reflection Paper

Have students write a reflection about their reading experiences as a culminating task for each marking period. If you want your students to produce reflection papers that are more structured, offer some guiding questions or key ideas they need to reflect on. You may choose to use the previous four steps as prompts (discuss difficulty, reading rate, favorite books, and goals) or scaffold the reflection paper to be more closely align to the individual goals you collaboratively set and discussed with your students.

Interactions with Others

You might choose to take a more collaborative approach to supporting students' reading. Start by planning a small-group format for book discussions: Choose whether you wish to establish book clubs, literature circles, online book discussions, or more informal book talks. Alternately, ask your students to decide what format they would prefer. See Figure 4.4 for how engaged students are when they have a routine that allows them to talk about books independently.

Figure 4.4 Students Engaged in a Book Discussion

Teacher-2-Teacher

I started a coffeehouse book chat routine in my class seven years ago. It occurs every Friday during the second quarter of the marking period. Room 213 becomes a bustling coffeehouse, complete with "coffee" (hot chocolate), bakery goods, and jazz music! The desks transform into coffee tables (about four to five "pods") with the lead book "chatter" seated at the head of each coffeehouse table. Several interactive book chats occur simultaneously around the classroom, and students rotate in eight-minute intervals to listen to new book chats (i.e., through discussion, presentation, and flyers) about the books their classmates are currently reading. I have found that if students take ownership of their learning, there will be an organic growth of skills as well as accelerated level of investment at the task(s) at hand.

Jessica Antonucci, middle school English teacher

 ## CHECK THIS OUT

Explore these resources on book clubs, literature circles, and other book discussion formats:

Books

Daniels H. 2002. *Literature Circles: Voice and Choice in Book Clubs & Reading Groups.* Portland, ME: Stenhouse.

Harvey D., and N. Steineke. 2004. *Mini-Lessons for Literature Circles.* Portsmouth, NH: Heinemann.

Kittle, P. 2013. *Book Love: Developing Depth, Stamina, and Passion in Adolescent Readers.* Portsmouth, NH: Heinemann.

Miller, D. 2009. *The Book Whisperer: Awakening the Inner Reader in Every Child.* San Francisco: Jossey-Bass.

O'Donnell-Allen, C. 2006. *The Book Club Companion: Fostering Strategic Readers in the Secondary Classroom.* Portsmouth, NH: Heinemann.

Moeller, V. J., and M. V. Moeller. 2001. *Socratic Seminars and Literature Circles for Middle School and High School English.* New York: Routledge.

———. 2007. *Literature Circles That Engage Middle and High School Students.* New York: Routledge.

Morganti, J. D. 2012. *Literature Circle Assessment Projects: Twenty Authentic, Engaging, and Ready-to-Use Activities to Assess and Reinforce Students' Understanding of Literature in Grades 4–8.* Seattle, WA: CreateSpace Independent Publishing Platform.

Blogs

Blogging Through the Fourth Dimension: http://pernillesripp.com

Mrs. Ripp Reads: https://rippreads.wordpress.com

NCTE High School Matters: http://nctesecondary.blogspot.com/

The Nerdy Teacher Blog: www.thenerdyteacher.com/

Three Teachers Talk Blog: https://threeteacherstalk.wordpress.com/

CELEBRATING AND SHARING READING

What research says about intrinsic motivation holds true for reading as well: The drive to accomplish something is much greater than any reward coming from the outside. When students dive into a book and do not want to stop reading, the reward is the book itself. Sharing what has had such an impact on the readers and celebrating reading accomplishments must be part of the reading routine you establish in the classroom. Sharing and celebrating may take a range of different forms; depending on the context, students can document their progress and quarterly outcomes and develop individual or group projects and other products.

Sharing Individual Reading Accomplishments Through Projects

One comprehensive approach to sharing individual outcomes is to create project-based responses. The style and scope of the project may vary depending on the grade level of your students and course content. Student ownership of the project is essential, so we encourage you to offer choices and to cultivate creative expressions. When Vaughan Danvers, middle school English as a second language teacher, studies the civil rights movement with her students through an extended unit, opportunities for deep thinking as well as creative expressions abound. Her class performs the play *The Brave Boys of Greensboro*, and each student creates his or her own mask as a graphic representation of the poem "We Wear the Mask" by Paul Laurence Dunbar. The masks in Figure 4.5a and 4.5b are a few of the results.

Figures 4.5a and 4.5b Student-Created Masks That Respond to Poetry

Teacher-2-Teacher

When I introduce the Chapter Graphics Project assignment, I ask my students to be "metaphorical photographers" and capture the quintessential "snapshot" of a chapter. Their goal is a complex one that takes about three to four class periods to complete. Working in pairs, students choose four important quotes from a chapter (representing parts of the text that are important in terms of character, big ideas, themes, author's craft, etc.), analyze how/why each quote is important (in other words, how the quote connects to the overall big idea of a text/character), sketch/draw an image (mentioned in the chapter) that could represent the chapter as a whole, and use at least three colors to illustrate the image— each color representing something intangible in the chapter (i.e., an important idea/ emotion/character trait, etc.). The colors must also be explained, and each graphic should feature a creative title that incorporates a literary device. (See Figures 4.6a and 4.6b for examples of Chapter Graphics Projects.)

Jessica Antonucci, middle school English teacher

Figures 4.6a and 4.6b Examples of Collaboratively Developed Chapter Graphics Projects

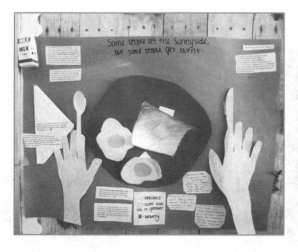

Individual or Group Presentations

Sharing may take many forms as well. If you implement an independent reading routine that also includes opportunities for students to work together, a group presentation or group sharing opportunity may be better suited.

Teacher-2-Teacher

At Alameda International High School, we introduced a routine that successfully gets students talking about books and reading. We call it the Great Literacy Poster Competition. At the end of each semester, students choose one of their favorite books and create a poster about it. We ask students to get across the basics about the book they chose in a creative way that will also get people to want to read the book. After the posters are hung, all the teachers trickle down to our wing to vote on the most successful posters. The rubric we design required the use of persuasion, creativity, and academic language. However, the best moments are when students from other classes stop and comment "I loved that book!" to no one in particular, or "I want to read that!" to a friend.

Josh Garfinkel, high school English language arts/English as a second language teacher

---

ROUTINE 2 Student-Directed Learning Routines

Stephanie Harvey and Anne Goudvis (2013) caution that "as teachers, we can flood the room with engaging texts, we can share interesting ideas, we can model our own curiosity, we can foster thoughtful conversations. Only they can turn what they hear, see, read, and talk about into knowledge by thinking deeply and expansively" (433). Adolescent learners are capable of thinking deeply and expansively, as long as they are given the opportunity to do so!

Some of the most frequently discussed concepts in nontraditional education are inquiry-based learning, project-based learning, personalized learning, and passion-based learning, each with its own unique set of characteristics, philosophies, and guidelines. (See the Check This Out section later in this chapter for some key resources.) Here we simply use the term *student-directed learning* to acknowledge the importance of a learner-centered approach that recognizes student autonomy and independence. Each of the routines shares an important teacher characteristic: the commitment to plan the task and support students (Schwartz 2015).

ANCHOR PROJECTS

Carol Ann Tomlinson (2001) was among the first to introduce the concept of anchoring. An anchor project allows students to remain focused on a topic of personal interest for a sustained length of time (often weeks, the entire marking period, or even the entire semester or year) after completing their assigned work. In a differentiated classroom, students will often complete assigned work at different times. Because all students are different, their assignments may vary as well. After modeling how to work on selected anchor activities, maintaining a portfolio, writing in a journal, reading a chosen book, practicing vocabulary with flashcards, and so on, your students should be prepared to automatically pick up their chosen ongoing project, without assistance from you.

Teacher-2-Teacher

We begin our public service announcement (PSA) project by asking students what they feel is the biggest problem facing the world today. Responses range from war and military conflicts around the world, pollution, obesity and fast food, and poverty to animal abuse, bullying, and climate change. The research becomes authentic since it stems from student inquiry.

Students are asked to produce a PSA that informs their audience about their issue. They create a photo story or Movie Maker video that incorporates a myriad of skills inherent in an English language arts curriculum, including research skills: paraphrasing, note taking, evaluating sources, creating citations. Additionally, students narrate their scripts, which must include valid research. While learning and using technology, students also evaluate the impact of the images they choose.

Having an anchor project that underlies the curriculum and addresses the skills presented makes the students more engaged each and every day. They recognize the importance of mastering the skills presented in the classroom because they want to create the best possible PSA. Students become self-motivated and engaged in the learning process (see Figure 4.7 for a student synopsis).

Heather Stumpf, middle school English teacher

Figure 4.7 A Seventh-Grade Student's Synopsis of Her PSA

What I liked about this PSA project was that I got to express something important to me. The point of this project was to inform others about a certain problem. I chose the topic of autism because it's a huge part of my life. My brother has autism. I did not only want to put facts about it here and there; I wanted to tell others that this is a growing issue and that we should care about the health of people with autism. I also wanted to show that even though someone may have more disadvantages than others, it is important to show compassion and respect toward them. I really enjoyed making this PSA and I hope it brought greater attention to this topic.

MINI–RESEARCH PROJECTS

Although an anchor project may span an entire marking period or even two marking periods, much shorter research projects may be designed to address an immediate question raised by students. Overnight, over a weekend, or within a few days, students can investigate their topic of interest. Invite your students to come back to class with the answer they have found to their mini-research questions and offer a brief report, a poster to be added to the bulletin board, or your class website.

PROJECT-BASED LEARNING

Project-based learning has been defined differently by different people. One definition comes from Thom Markham (2012), who emphasized that project-based learning is a problem-solving process, the goal of which is for students to show mastery. However, mastery is demonstrated not just in the form of a final product but by identifying and elaborating on the steps students took to create the project.

The shared focus among all educators who use projects in their courses is the marked departure from traditional, teacher-directed learning. Instead, these teachers facilitate student-generated exploration: Students identify the process they will take to reach an answer and produce a final product as the outcome of their work. Projects may be extended to any grade level and any content area. See Figure 4.8, for a student's response to the Egg Drop Challenge from Carrie McDermott and Ken Giosi's collaborative sixth-grade science class. The task is for students to figure out how to drop a container (with an egg inside) from the second-floor fire escape and ensure that it remains unharmed. Students apply their knowledge about Newton's laws of motion to assist them in their design. They write a description of their container and why they used specific features to protect the egg, while explaining Newton's laws in their description and explanation.

Figure 4.8 Egg Drop Project Student Work

Franky   1-1
Dr. Mc.Demmot.   Science

    Newtons laws in an egg project.

    I will be writing about how Newtons
laws are in the egg project.Newton's laws
are in everything we do in life.Newtons
laws are very important. For example, if
we didn't have Newton's laws we
would not be able to figure how much
force people apply to an object.
    My egg project is an egg in
a grocery bag.Then I add 14 more
bags to make a total of 15 bags wrapped
around the egg to make a ball shape.
When I'm finished with the ball shape
I added a big pearashoot show it
would go down slower and have a
softer landing.I used the grocery bags
because they are like cotton ball in a ball-
oon and the bag have some air so it
would kinda be like a pearashoot
and slow the egg.Inertia would also
slow down the egg.If I use lots of
force the egg would probualy break
but.If I let it go without using lots

force I would have a 99% chance
of not breaking.
    As you can see that Newton's
laws are very important to our
lifes.without Newton's laws we would
not be able to do projects like the
egg project without knowing whats going
on.With the Newtons laws we can
figure out how much force we apply
to an object and how fast its traveling.
If Newton wasn't born would we
be able to figure what is motion,
force, balanced force,unbalanced force,
Inertia, and more.

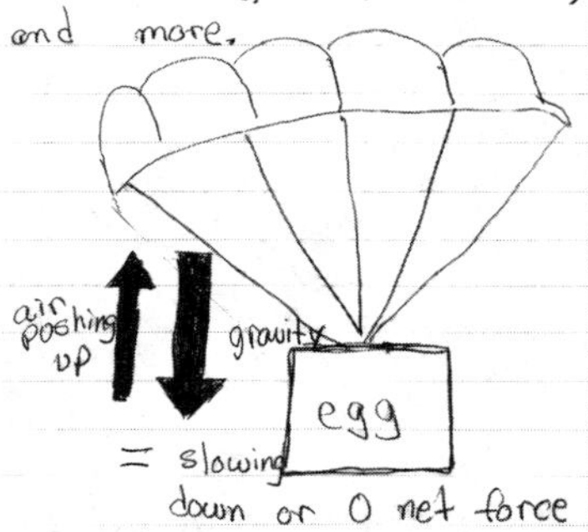

air pushing up   gravity   egg

= slowing
down or 0 net force

Teacher-2-Teacher

In our cotaught sixth-grade social studies class, inquiry-based learning projects are used to help students understand challenging concepts. We pose questions, which allow our students to discover, question, and draw conclusions. In this project, students were having difficulty understanding how people moved from Paleolithic to Neolithic times. Stations were set up, and students had to "gather," "hunt," or "build permanent shelters." Each scenario led to a problem, for example: "You have to hunt for buffalo. Walk around the room and look for buffalo. You need seven buffalo to have enough to feed the entire clan. What problem do you notice?" Students noticed they did not have enough food to survive or were not able to build a permanent shelter. Through synthesis, students were able to explain how farming and agriculture impacted the development of the Paleolithic era from the Neolithic era. See Figure 4.9 picturing student collaboration in this hands-on, minds-on learning task.

    Vanessa Kittilsen and James Schneider, middle school coteachers

Figure 4.9 Students Engaged in an Inquiry-Based Learning Project

COACH'S NOTES

When students work in project-based learning teams, one of the best ways to assess team health and wellness are weekly "status" updates, especially for long-term projects. The project Gantt chart (see http://teamgantt.com) visually documents progress and keeps team members accountable to share the work as well as offers natural practice on presentation and critiquing skills. Students prepare a ten-minute Google presentation that identifies the problem they are trying to solve through a design thinking challenge— the framework we used most often for project-based learning. Students show how they used design methods to identify problems, build empathy, iterate design solutions, and prepare final prototypes to meet user needs. This "status" update routine keeps students accountable, beats team issues before they happen, and provides the class an opportunity for peer learning.

Lisa M. Abel-Palmieri, Ph.D.,
Director of Technology and Innovation

CHECK THIS OUT

Inquiry-based or project-based learning rests on the foundation of student collaboration. Explore seminal and current work on project-based learning in the following:

Books

Bender, W. N. 2012. *Project-Based Learning: Differentiating Instruction for the 21st Century.* Thousand Oaks, CA: Corwin Press.

Krauss, J. I., and S. K. Boss. 2013. *Thinking Through Project-Based Learning: Guiding Deeper Inquiry.* Thousand Oaks, CA: Corwin Press.

Laur, D. 2013. *Authentic Learning Experiences: A Real-World Approach to Project-Based Learning.* New York: Routledge.

McKenzie, W. N. 2012. *Intelligence Quest: Project-Based Learning and Multiple Intelligences.* Waynesville, NC: International Society for Technology in Education

Websites

Edutopia Resources on project-based learning: www.edutopia.org/project-based-learning

Buck Institute for Education: http://bie.org

PBS Online professional development on inquiry-based learning: www.thirteen.org/edonline/concept2class/inquiry/index.html

Video Clips

Buck Institute YouTube channel: www.youtube.com/user/BIEPBL

GENIUS HOUR OR INNOVATION DAY ROUTINES

Educators around the country have been inspired by a recent wave of innovation in the business world famously referred to as the Genius Hour, FedEx Day, or Innovation Day. Google is well known to require (not merely allow) its employees to spend 20 percent of their workweek (an entire day) to an idea they are personally vested in and want to further develop. FedEx Day—though its name is misleading—did not originate with the shipping company FedEx; it was actually used as a metaphor for fast delivery or overnight delivery of an innovation.

The notion that employees spend a certain amount of their work day or workweek to develop an innovation they are passionate about resulted in high levels of productivity and new development of products around the globe. Daniel Pink (2009) discusses why these initiatives are so successful and concludes that people are allowed to use their autonomy, work toward a purpose, and reach mastery.

As documented on his blog, Josh Stumpenhorst (2013), a sixth-grade language arts and social science teacher at Lincoln Junior High School in Naperville, Illinois, transferred the concept of Innovation Days based on Daniel Pink's (2009) work from the business context to education. Since then, teachers nationally and internationally have embarked on similar ventures. See Figure 4.10 for Tyler Messman and April D'Water's joint letter to secure parental support for their Genius Hour

Project facilitated collaboratively in their middle school English language arts and social studies classes. Figure 4.11 pictures one of their students at Genius Night presenting her project on organizing a drive to gather school supplies for students who cannot afford them, and Figure 4.12 depicts the advertising poster she created to get support from her schoolmates and the community.

Figure 4.10 Parent Information Letter About the Genius Hour Passion Project

Dear Buccaneer Families,

We are very excited to share a great new idea we are trying to implement in both English and social studies classes. The idea is called "Genius Hour" and is based off of an idea Google created: employees received 20 percent of their time each week to work on a project that was a passion of theirs. This idea has been gaining momentum in schools around the nation. Students will come up with a project and presentation idea. Working to improve our lives through research based on our interests is at the heart of Genius Hour Passion Projects. They will be working on their Genius Hour projects every Friday alternating between English and Social Studies. Genius Hour is a privilege that can be taken away due to behavior and/or failing grades as determined by the teachers.

Here are the guidelines:

- Every Friday will be designated as Genius Hour during one class period.
- Students are allowed to work on a project of their choosing and it should be something they are passionate about.
- The Genius Hour topic must be approved by Mr. Messman or Ms. D'Water by Halloween.
- Students must conduct adequate research on their topic.
- Students must produce a product or achieve a goal.
- Projects should be geared toward bettering themselves, the school, the community, or the world.
- Students must blog weekly about their project to reflect on the process.
- Students should meet with Mr. Messman or Ms. D'Water when they get stuck.
- Students will present their final project to the community at the end of the semester.

We are asking that you help your child brainstorm and select an idea. We cannot wait to see students discover their inner genius as their projects unfold.

Thank you,
Mr. Messman and Ms. D'Water

Figure 4.11 Student Presenting Her Genius Project at Genius Night

Figure 4.12 A Student's Poster to Advertise Her Project

> ### School Supply Drive!
>
> - Help support our Prentice Elementary, Middle, and High School to collect supplies for our classes.
> - Please bring in some supplies and drop in a bin around the community.
> - Throughout the year there will be boxes for supplies to be put in (Community Bank, Hardware Store, Prentice IGA).
> - My goal is to have a day set in 2015 at the beginning of the school year for supplies to be picked out when needed.
> - Please do not take advantage of this. I am trying to help ones that cannot afford supplies.
> - I will be collecting supplies during this school year for the beginning of next year!

SOLE

SOLE (self-organized learning environment) is an exciting global project and classroom practice that is being supported by the TED community (a nonprofit devoted to sharing ideas from the technology, entertainment, and design worlds, that has expanded to include the educational world). Requiring only one laptop per four students, SOLEs engage students to research their own questions, or questions that you might pose at first. Requiring Internet research and group presentations, SOLEs encourage collaboration among group members, as well as self-directed learning. See http://tedsole.tumblr.com for your students to join the global SOLE community and to share photos and comments from your own SOLE experiences to the Tumblr website!

GAMES FOR LEARNING

Games play a critical role in many adolescents' lives and their socialization process. James Gee (2003) was among the first to research the impact video games have on youngsters' language and literacy development, claiming that games contribute significantly to academic skills. Gamers read complex, technical texts (manuals, gaming cheat sheets, etc.) and develop robust vocabulary in the process.

Video games are known to be highly motivating, as players meet incrementally harder challenges, build new skills, and move from level to level. In a *gamified classroom* teachers can create a similar experience for students in which a mastery system is implemented: Students get hints and cues as well as partial solutions (otherwise known as *scaffolds*) until they progress to the next level of understanding and skill until mastery is reached.

Many teachers use games in traditional or more updated formats to appeal to students' desire to engage in a gamelike activity. Teachers might present a generic or discipline-specific challenge to their students for which they design a game. Teachers might challenge students to solve a survival game or engage in other gamelike activities in which difficult concepts are explored without the traditional paper-and-pencil or chalk-and-talk format.

Lee Mattes, a high school chemistry teacher, presents a different project or game in each quarter to his tenth graders to connect the curriculum to the outside world. His students respond especially well to his invitation to

Figure 4.13 Mole Day Project: A Lollipop Plant

celebrate National Mole Day (www.moleday.org) by creating a project that signifies how large the mole number is. Mole Day was created to generate interest in chemistry; it commemorates the number (6.02×10^{23}), which is a basic measuring unit in chemistry, called the Mole. Mr. Mattes is not alone; schools around the United States celebrate Mole Day with various chemistry activities. See Figure 4.13 for a student's Mole Day project: The lollipop plant, a gift to the Mole, was accompanied by the student's calculations of how many years it would take to lick a mole number of lollipops if we could finish 2,000 lollipops per second.

Jordan Shapiro (2014) recognizes the choices teachers make through gamification: Grades may be replaced with levels and merit badges and lectures replaced with project-based units where completion, or the demonstration of mastery, allows students to move on. He claims that "when learning is structured like a game, students intuitively understand the cumulative nature of learning. They're motivated to master a compounding sequence of skills" (paragraph 7).

Creating games that are tied to the course objectives and course content is another highly engaging activity teachers have utilized. Yet the rigorous demands of the current standards might leave some teachers puzzled over how to keep games a manageable and meaningful part of their teaching. See Figure 4.14a and 4.14b for excerpts from Brooke Feldman's project-planning direction sheet, which specifies how students are expected to design a board game that includes the rigor and relevance of the Common Core State Standards (National Governor's Association Center for Best Practices and Council of Chief State School Officers 2010) while also challenging students to be innovative and original.

Teacher-2-Teacher

There are some activities students love. For my students, it's anything that involves competition, creativity, and control over their own learning. So it's no surprise that my board game project is a success every year. I ask students to work as teams to create original games that help them review Indian history and religion for our unit exam. I dedicate multiple class periods and provide the materials students need to build their games. After writing the rules, designing the games, and testing their creations, the students compete to sell their products. They create sales pitches to argue their games' uniqueness, engagement, and historical accuracy. Then, all students get a chance to play each other's games. In all, this project is rigorous and engaging, and truly helps students cultivate ownership over their learning. Brooke Feldman, middle school English and social studies teacher

Figure 4.14a Indian History and Religion Board Game Project (Excerpts from Brooke Feldman's Project Planning Direction Sheet)

The goal of this assignment is to create an interactive, engaging board game through which you identify and explain the important events, ideas, people, and places in Indian history. The board game will count as a 75-point minor assessment grade for third quarter.

Game Requirements

Inside your game box, you need:

1. Instructions (How do you play? What is required? What is the goal?)
2. A decorated board game (color, illustrations/graphics)
3. Thirty question cards with answers on the back (submitted in a bag or envelope)
4. Tokens or game pieces
5. A method for moving the pieces around the game board (dice, spinner, drawing cards, etc.)

Question Card Requirements

Indian Religions:

You must incorporate *at least* five of the terms from *each* religion (fifteen total):

Hinduism	Buddhism	Islam
• Atman	• Eightfold Path	• Allah
• Brahma, Vishnu, Shiva	• Four Noble Truths	• Five Pillars of Islam
• Caste System	• Meditation	• Hajj
• Karma	• Reincarnation	• Mohammad
• Moksha	• Siddhartha	• Mecca and Medina
• Reincarnation		• Qu'ran
• Samsara		• Ramadan

Indian History:

You must incorporate *at least five* of the terms from *each* time period (fifteen total):

Mughal Empire	British Raj	Modern India
• Akbar the Great • Aurangzeb • Jahangir • Shah Jahan • Taj Mahal	• Colonialism • Imperialism • Industrialization • Mahatma Gandhi • Positive and negative impacts of British rule • Satyagraha	• India and Pakistan • Indian Independence Act • Jawaharlal Nehru • Partition • World War II

Bonus Point Opportunity

You can receive 1 bonus point for every primary source successfully used. Just asking "Who wrote _____?" doesn't cut it. Rather, the source and its content must be incorporated into the questions and/or game. You can earn a maximum of 5 bonus points.

For more information on Ms. Feldman's approach to using board games:
https://coretransition.wordpress.com/2015/02/06/board-games-2-0-updating-a-popular-project-so-it-meets-common-core

Figure 4.14b Student-Created Board Game

Outside-the-Classroom Routines

Marilyn M. Lombardi (2007) defines authentic learning as one that "typically focuses on real-world, complex problems and their solutions, using role-playing exercises, problem-based activities, case studies, and participation in virtual communities of practice" (3). Although authentic learning can be designed to take place in the classroom, one overlooked territory for learning is outside the school. Washor and Mojkowski (2013) suggest that *leaving-to-learn opportunities*—such as internships, travel, community service, work, entrepreneurial ventures, and gap years" (xxvii)—should be an integral part of all students' education. The main argument for such experiences is that students learn at the "edge of their competence" as they draw on the world outside school and bring new learning and accomplishments back to school.

SERVICE-LEARNING (COMMUNITY ENGAGEMENT)

Some schools require an out-of-class service learning or authentic learning experience to be carried out, documented, and submitted for credit. Others make it an optional, enrichment opportunity. By definition, "service learning is a learning tool to empower students to solve problems in their communities, or even globally. It is a student-driven process, where students learn about a particular issue, place, or problem, then figure out how to take action in a positive way" (Farber 2011, 5). Service learning fosters student creativity and autonomy, while enhancing students' sense of dignity and self-efficacy as they make a difference in other people's lives. Consider the following steps to design a service-learning component in your secondary class:

- Examine your course content and curricular needs.
- Invite others to form a service-learning team.
- Find community members or local experts to support the initiative.
- Design the service-learning project.
- Identify needed resources.
- Plan for a culminating event.
- Assess civic responsibility and set up student presentations.
- Save time for reflection.

Here are some discipline-specific suggestions on some feasible service learning projects possibilities:

Science
- Local habitat preservation (teams assess and teach about a local habitat).

Language Arts, English, and Literacy
- Create a newspaper or magazine for your community, with all the parts.

Math
- Interview local professionals who use math in their jobs. Create a community resource (book, website, guide, etc.) and share.

Social Studies

- Create new legislation to solve a community problem. Take it to the local legislator or the capital of your state to share.

Art

- Find a community need for art: a mural in an alley, hospital or clinic, rundown area of town, or on the side of the school. Work together to create it.
- Create an art show for an approved charity. Create art to sell in an evening community event to raise funds for the charity (or your school).

Physical Education

- Interview the staff of a school about their exercise habits. Create a movie, book, or website to share with the school community.

Adapted from Katy Farber (2011)

FIELD TRIPS AND GUEST SPEAKERS

In recent years, field trips and out-of-school explorations started to diminish due to budgetary restrictions and student safety concerns. Yet, firsthand experiences—visits to local museums, science labs, or animal shelters, or places much further away from home such as the backstage of a Broadway theater in New York City or the Smithsonian museums in Washington, DC, historical sites, battlefields, monuments, national parks, science centers—not only engage students for the day but may have a life-changing impact. They can lead to career choices, increased civic engagement, and volunteerism. Recent research has documented that students who saw live theater demonstrated "enhanced knowledge of the plot and vocabulary in those plays, greater tolerance, and improved ability to read the emotions of others" (Greene et al. 2015, 55). Similarly, students who visit an art museum not only develop more knowledge about art, they also "have stronger critical-thinking skills, exhibit increased historical empathy, display higher levels of tolerance, and have a greater taste for consuming art and culture" (Greene, Kisida, and Bowen 2014, 80). Based on your community, other cultural institutions or STEM (science, technology, engineering, and mathematics)-based experiences should also be considered.

Teacher-2-Teacher

One of my favorite trips is Technology Day at Adventureland Amusement Park in Farmingdale, New York, so my eighth-grade students can see math in action. Prior to the event, we review old concepts and introduce new ones. We discuss the many careers involving mathematics that can be found at the amusement park: engineering (mechanical, electrical), business as owner/manager, accounting, and marketing.

On the day of the trip, students enthusiastically board the bus for Adventureland. Groups of ten students choose five rides to observe and analyze. For example, one group looks at the Ferris wheel ride and ramp and become engineers for the day to see if the ride could be made handicap accessible. Students gain a sense of service, which gives meaning to their mathematical task. Some of the questions they need to consider are the length of the ramp, the given space, the time allotted to load and unload the passengers from the ride, the safety of the passengers, and the size of the cabin of the Ferris wheel. Students sketch what the ramp should look like and calculate the height, length, and angle of elevation using trigonometry.

Favorite rides include the Music Express, the Pirate Ship, and the Wave Swing. Each ride offers a new learning experience, whether it's calculating RPM (revolutions per minute) or understanding the use of a level. By the end of the day, students not only become aware of the safety features of the rides and the structures themselves, they see the "word problem" from the textbook come to life.

Ellen Van Wie, high school mathematics teacher

When field trips are not feasible, the world can enter the classroom by way of guest speakers or virtual visitors who join the class session for a short period of time. Guest speakers offer a unique perspective to augment the curriculum and to bring the community into the classroom. Try https://education.skype.com/literacy to set up a Skype session with an author. Teachers around the country have been supporting each other by creating a Twitter list of children's book and young adult authors (#RockStarAuthors) who respond to classroom invitations and do Skype sessions with classes for no fee. For example, you may contact the following authors:

Middle School
- Tricia Springstubb (*Moonpenny Island, Cody and the Fountain of Happiness*)
- Eric Luper (*Jeremy Bender vs. the Cupcake Cadets, Seth Baumgartner's Love Manifesto*)
- Chris Grabenstein (*The Island of Dr. Libris, Escape from Mr. Lemoncello's Library*)
- C. Alexander (*Tides of War, Dog Tags*)

High School
- Debby Dahl Edwardson (*My Name Is Not Easy, Blessing's Bead*)
- Mary Rose Wood (*My Life the Musical, Why I Let My Hair Grow Out*)
- Peter Adam Salomon (*Henry Franks, All Those Broken Angels*)

Teacher-2-Teacher

I like inviting guest speakers into my high school business class to share their experiences in the real world with my students. So far, we've had an assistant district attorney, a county police officer, a tax volunteer coordinator, and a human resources manager from a big box retailer speak to the students about different careers. I plan to invite an FBI agent, another parent of one of my students later this year, as well as industry professionals. My students really enjoy having the guest speakers. I prepare students beforehand so they are familiar

SHARED FAMILY LEARNING EXPERIENCES

Regardless of the content area you teach, think of ways to encourage shared learning experience that your students and their families can participate in. If you teach English language arts, social studies, or visual or performing arts, you can encourage your students seek out local cultural experiences, historical locations, library talks, or musical and dance performances that they would like to share with family members and have them report on it for extra credit. If you teach math, science, or technical subjects, suggest STEM-related lectures or other local events to your students to consider. You know your community, but your students and their families might not be always be aware of what is available in terms of family engagement, so make suggestions or maintain a Web page with links to where they can go. If you require one of these visits per quarter, your website or a class blog could include a photo of the student's visit and a short review of the experience to motivate other students to try the same.

Teacher-2-Teacher

The arts are the physical manifestation of our collective culture. In today's world of modern technology, students have unprecedented access to information and unlimited exposure to art in all of its forms; however, a student cannot have a moving personal experience with an art form when it is compacted onto a tablet or smartphone screen. By encouraging students to attend cultural events (concerts, theatrical productions, dance showcases, galleries, museums, etc.) and then requiring them to reflect on their experiences, not only will students gain a deeper understanding of the art, but they will become culturally versatile. These personal cultural experiences will forever assist students by giving them the prior knowledge necessary to aid them when studying a literary work or historical event by allowing them to accurately visualize settings, deeply comprehend characters' and people's actions and responses to conflicts, and thoroughly grasp the greater themes that define the human experience.

Edward Grosskreutz, high school English teacher

Special Considerations

Learning to become more authentic and designing more individualized assignments would be no small feat if you worked with only with a small number of students each day. The realities of the secondary school context require careful consideration and thoughtful planning of how to make sure students receive such instruction in every marking period. See the following suggestions.

What if you teach over 100 students each day?

Planning, supporting, monitoring, and assessing student-directed work when you see over 100 students a day might be a challenge, yet many of the routines we described in this chapter are manageable because they provide a system that students can learn to run on their own. When you facilitate small groups rather than addressing the entire class from the front of the room for an entire period, you'll find that you get to know your students better as you interact with them. This will lead to better classroom management when you are back to whole-class instruction. Several of the routines we suggest should be established as group projects that call for student collaboration, thus reducing the number of submissions you will need to review and assess. At the same time, inviting students to work together for a common goal and expecting them to establish their own routines for collaboration will help build several critical twenty-first-century skills: creativity and innovation, critical thinking and problem solving, communication and collaboration (www.p21.org).

What if you teach multiple courses each semester?

Depending on the course content, authentic learning opportunities will vary. To make sure you can manage the variety of projects and independent work that is going on, we suggest you maintain a solid organizational system. You might choose something as simple as Google Calendar or as complex as an e-portfolio.

If you designate times for project work, such as Innovation Days or Genius Hours, make sure this type of routine is not scheduled at the same time in all of your classes. Create a calendar that clearly indicates the beginning and end dates of each quarterly routine to avoid confusion. You may also decide that only one or two routines will be utilized in your classes per course; quarterly routines are among the most manageable types of routines.

What if you don't have your own classroom?

Most of the practices presented in this chapter require students to complete a project or engage in a learning task independently or in groups, or even outside the school day, so they can be accomplished without the consistency of having your own classroom. Carefully select the materials and resources to be used for any authentic learning routines that are connected to classroom space. Take advantage of cloud storage that allows resources to be retrieved digitally from any location, such as Dropbox or Google Drive. Alternately, maintain a course website preloaded with links and other digital files that students can access. An electronic progress monitoring system (Google Docs or Google Forms) of student work eliminates the need for transferring hard copies from room to room.

What if your class period is longer than the typical forty- to forty-four-minute class?

If your typical class period takes sixty minutes or longer, additional class time may be reserved for independent reading, conferring with students individually or in small groups, planning and discussing the project students are working on, or student presentations on the outcome of the projects.

The commitment to authentic learning tasks will require face-to-face guidance and class time that you might more willingly carve out if you have block scheduling in your building.

What if you want to incorporate technology?

Create a class website that provides students and their parents with all the necessary information:

- **detailed description of the goals and expectations**
- **step-by-step directions or other scaffolds for students who need more structure and support to be able to meet the requirements**
- **project completion time lines including checkpoints and due dates**
- **assessment tools such as rubrics for transparency and clarity of expectations.**

Technology tools and Web-based resources support authentic learning opportunities. Tablets, iPads, and laptops give access to the Internet to locate information and to create new knowledge. Here are a few of our favorite sites:

1. Use this interactive map to see where educators around the United States take their students on a field trip and why: www.edweek.org/tm/section/community/field-trip-map.html.
2. Follow Captain Barrington Irving and his crew on www.flyingclassroom.com as they embark on a global journey connected to STEM curricula.
3. Visit the Florida Center for Instructional Technology at http://fcit.usf.edu to locate a vast collection of online resources that support authentic Web-based explorations.
4. Use the street view of www.googlemaps.com for global geographical explorations.
5. Browse websites that offer access to authentic digital content to support history and social studies course content: explore Digital History at www.digitalhistory.uh.edu/copyright.cfm or the Library of Congress at www.loc.gov, or have students make time lines at www.timetoast.com and create other digital products.
6. Participate in the annual Global Read Aloud initiated by Pernille Ripp, a seventh-grade teacher from Oregon, Wisconsin. Since 2010, more than 10,000 facilitators have read aloud to over 500,000 students. Join her at www.globalreadaloud.com.

A Final Thought

Reading for joy and excitement and engaging in research that addresses authentic issues and problems identified by students have a documented positive impact on their academic and social development. These learning experiences are driven by students' own choices and inquisitiveness. Guest speakers, field trips, community involvement, and service learning are just a few ways schools may provide secondary students with out-of-school experiences that are not only connected to the curriculum, but also nurture their curiosity to explore topics of interest and their desire to be engaged in the community.

Essential Questions for Individual Reflection, Collegial Circles, and Group Discussions

- *What is the central idea running through this chapter that informs your instruction?*

- *Why is it important to provide ample opportunity for your students to read independently?*

- *How will you fit the recommended routines into your quarterly plans?*

- *How often do students engage in authentic research projects in your course? How often should they or could they be doing so?*

- *What challenges do you anticipate as you implement the suggested routines for each marking period?*

- *How can you support your students to pursue their own inquiries?*

- *How can you challenge advanced learners while continuing to provide support for on-grade learners as well as struggling learners?*

All is well that ends well.

Proverb

Chapter 5

END-OF-COURSE ROUTINES

Too many people dream of the results of success and ignore the process.

Tom Morris (2002, 63)

Overview

In this chapter, we

- summarize research support for the routines we present
- establish routines for the end of your course
- present examples, templates, resources, and classroom vignettes along with recommendations from coaches to support the implementation of end-of-course routines
- discuss special considerations for variations in teaching assignments (large number of students, multiple courses or multiple sections of the same course, varied lengths of class periods) and technology integration.

End-of-Course Routines at a Glance

ROUTINE 1 -- -- ➤ **Routines for Synthesizing Course Learning**

Review Routines
- Jigsaw Review
- Application Routines

Alternative Assessment Routines
- Student-Generated Assessments
- Final Projects
- Portfolios

ROUTINE 2 -- -- ➤ **Routines for Reflection and Celebration of Learning**

Self-Examination Routines
- Self-Evaluation and Goal Setting

Creative Expressions
- Memoir Writing
- Letter to Freshmen
- Video
- End-of-Year Celebration

What Does the Research Say About the Role of Review, Self-Assessment, Alternative Assessment, and Reflection?

If we as educators agree that one of the major purposes of secondary schooling is to internalize, transfer, and apply learning to future situations and new problems, we must also be deliberate about how we evaluate students' ability to transfer and apply what they have learned to new contexts. In *How People Learn*, Bransford, Brown, and Cocking (2004) suggest that the transfer of learning is an active process; it should not be evaluated by one-time tests (even though it seems to be a very common practice at the end of the school year when finals are given). Instead, they emphasize that "students develop flexible understanding of when, where, why, and how to use their knowledge to solve new problems if they learn how to extract underlying themes and principles from their learning exercises. Understanding how and when to put knowledge to use . . . is an important characteristic of expertise" (236). When students are provided with opportunities to synthesize what they have learned in a new way, their engagement with the content is further enhanced. When they can reflect on their learning and practice transfer through varied modes of assessments that focus on application of knew knowledge and skills, their retention increases.

Hattie (2012) emphasized the importance of giving students opportunities to reflect on and predict their performance. He noted that "educating students to have high, challenging, appropriate expectation is among the most powerful influence in enhancing student achievement" (54). He further noted that teachers should pay attention to a range of self-processes such as self-goals, self-dependence, and self-efficacy.

End-of-Course Routines

You are more than likely to devote some special time at the end of the year to reviewing course content. Based on local and state regulations, you are also likely to have a final exam or a performance-based assessment as a requirement for course completion. We believe in giving students additional opportunities to bring closure to the course, such as allowing them to select from a choice of meaningful, engaging routines. In this chapter, we recommend end-of-course routines for consolidating and reflecting upon learning. To build and strengthen school culture, Ronald Williamson and Barbara Blackburn (2009a) suggested that school leaders see the end of the year as a time for celebrating success and laying the groundwork for the upcoming school year. Similarly, each teacher can take time to celebrate the success in the classroom and to set the tone for future learning. Although we recognize that the end-of-course/end-of year time is busy with a range of demands, be sure to include a few end-of-year routines that will bring closure to your students' learning experience. It will allow them to reflect on what they have accomplished, recognize challenges they have faced, and determine goals for self-improvement going forward.

ROUTINE **1** **Routines for Synthesizing Course Learning**

As your course draws to a close, it's important to review and synthesize essential information. Choose one or more of the review routines and alternative assessment routines from the selection presented here, keeping in mind that your course content, the age and grade level of your students might determine which practice yields the best results.

REVIEW ROUTINES

Although teacher-created learning packets or review sheets are common, there are other ways to ensure your students review essential learning and core skills from your course. The two review routines we suggest here are (1) a jigsaw activity that utilizes small-group configurations and student collaboration, and (2) an application routine that calls for transferring new knowledge and skills acquired in the course to new contexts and authentic situations.

Jigsaw Review

Why not shift the major responsibility for reviewing at the end of the year from teacher to student? You can present students with an overarching outline of key concepts and topics, turning-point events, and big ideas. After that, let them take ownership for reviewing the content of your course.

Group students for collaboration and have each group create a two- to three-page review (adding details to the outline) on a major concept, topic, turning point, or big idea. Encourage students to use color, bold print, boxes, and other text features to sort and classify information to make the review notes more accessible to others. Have each group include visuals that will trigger recall of important information. Together, they will cocreate a class review booklet titled *Everything You Ever Wanted to Know About (add your class title here).*

This jigsaw writing task can be followed up with a presentation by each of the "group experts." During this interactive study review, you will be able to add to the conversation, clarify misconceptions, and fortify student understanding.

Although each group is responsible for one or two sections of the outline, all students will receive a copy of the booklet. These student-generated study notes can be photocopied or placed in a Google Doc for everyone to access. Yes, you will probably want to review the notes before making this booklet available to all. However, weigh the benefits: The process of creating one's own notes is a powerful tool for student learning. There will be more engagement if students are responsible for the study process. For once, your students will be working harder than you are during the review.

Application Routines

How many times have you heard your students say, "Why do we need to learn this? Will I ever use this in real life?" Here is an opportunity to turn this question around at the end of your course and ask your students to answer their own questions. Applying knowledge and skills to new situations and transferring them to a new context represents a high-level cognitive challenge for most students. Shana Carpenter (2012) affirms that "transfer may be considered the ultimate goal of learning, given that in everyday life, the context in which learned information must be utilized is likely to differ from that in which it was originally acquired" (1). Within the context of teaching authentic language arts and content-based literacy skills in a test-driven era, Arthur Costigan (2008) advocates for engaging students in meaningful learning experiences that are authentic and reality-based.

First, create an outline or graphic organizer depicting your entire course. Try to be selective and include just the most important "big ideas." Make it look like a navigational tool, a flowchart, or a mind map of the course. Alternately, invite your students to cocreate this course map so they have even more ownership of the next steps in the routine. Remind them to identify broad-based, essential concepts and important skills they have learned. They will exercise their critical thinking skills at the highest possible levels of synthesis and evaluation as they make their selections.

In small groups, students examine the course map or a small part of it and identify as many real-life connections and applications as possible. Initially, encourage students to focus on familiar contexts, such as current events or personal experiences. These may include but not be limited to their home life, hobbies, sports, and jobs they might have as teenagers. For example, in a geometry class, students will make connections to household activities such as gardening, putting in a flower bed, building a birdhouse, and so on. In social studies, students may transfer learned concepts for any historical era to current events taking place locally, regionally, nationally, or globally. In an English language arts class, the major themes discussed in the readings may be connected to students' own experiences in life. Or, students may examine the types of conflicts or choices characters had to make and then compare these literary examples to their own lives.

Having first identified the connections between the course content and their own day-to-day experiences, they are ready to apply new learning to much broader contexts. If students are ready to be challenged, more elaborate applications may be encouraged: citizenship, civic responsibilities, participation in the workforce, construction, transportation.

ALTERNATIVE ASSESSMENT ROUTINES

How can we mitigate the overreliance on paper-and-pencil tests at the end of the school year? In Chapter 3 we discussed alternative assessment routines utilized at the end of a unit. Similarly, students can demonstrate mastery of course content through alternative ways. Performance-based assessments are designed to engage students.

Student-Generated Assessments

Not only can student-generated, authentic questions be the driving force behind a review activity, they can also be used as a highly motivating way to add student input into a more formal assessment. By the time students start middle school or high school, they have taken a lot of tests. They have a solid understanding of and practice with responding to multiple-choice questions, short-response and extended-response questions, and essay prompts, as well as a range of content-specific tasks. But how many assessments have they contributed to? When students have been taught to ask their own high-level questions about a topic, concept, or idea, greater understanding is the result. Why not encourage their questioning by choosing to use a few of the best questions contributed by students on an upcoming formal assessment? See Figure 5.1 for student-generated essay questions for a tenth-grade social studies class.

Figure 5.1 Student-Generated Essay Questions, Tenth Grade

What are some implications of World War II that we can still see today?

How are World War I and World War II similar and different?

Final Projects

We discussed projects within the context of creating routines for each marking period in Chapter 4 even though project-based learning is practiced by many as a student-centered exploration throughout the entire year. Whether it is a sustained approach or an occasional practice, an end-of-course culminating project serves as a vehicle to synthesize and evaluate learning outcomes. Students demonstrate what they have learned through the year by completing a single comprehensive project as illustrated in the following Teacher-2-Teacher.

Teacher-2-Teacher

June is a milestone month. Although our end-of-year projects often vary according to the texts and journeys we've taken throughout the school year, they mostly involve galleries—showcases proudly demonstrating the depth and scope of our learning. Galleries are final opportunities to exhibit how students have built upon and expanded their abilities as readers, writers, and thinkers. One example is our Interdisciplinary Gallery. We reserve a special, public area in the school and transform the space into a three-day museum exhibit! Their work is on display for teachers, administrators, and peers. The Interdisciplinary Gallery is a complex project that asks students to identify a big idea *(connected to both their English and social studies classes), then* create an open-ended question *connected to this big idea, and finally* create a project *that seeks to present the "answer" to the question (see Figure 5.2 for further clarification). The "answer" portion of this project is essentially what is presented in the gallery and represents some type of tangible outcome to the questions. The projects run the gamut—poster boards, videos, models/displays, artwork, original music, websites/blogs, animation, and even student-made, playable, video games!*

Jessica Antonucci, middle school English language arts teacher

Portfolios

Portfolios are the hallmark presentation tool in many professions. A student portfolio is a collection of student work that represents his or her literacy and content-related activities, accomplishments, and achievements. Process portfolios contain work samples that document growth over time, while end-of-year portfolios or product portfolios demonstrate mastery of course content and contain only their best work (Venn 2007). You can choose to implement portfolio assessment in your own classroom, or you can involve your colleagues in designing a grade-level, department-wide, or school-wide approach to this form of assessment.

For example, when you decide to create a portfolio assessment for an English class, consider including some of the following items:

- letter to the reader introducing what is included in the portfolio
- quotations that have special meaning for the student
- sample paragraphs that illustrate writing techniques and crafts
- sample essays of various types (descriptive, narrative, explanatory, expository, persuasive, cause and effect, compare and contrast, and others)
- sample of written work from other classes (lab reports, speech outlines, summaries, essays, projects).

Figure 5.2 Student Directions and Project Checklist for the Interdisciplinary Gallery

The **Interdisciplinary Gallery** is an important, final opportunity to exhibit your thoughts on how the texts we read in English class thematically connect to the events in our nation's past and present.

The chart below is a brief overview of the Interdisciplinary Gallery; it will give you a snapshot of the details and important elements of this project.

BIG ideas	Identify the BIG Question	Choose Your Presentation Format	Requirements
Conflict Challenge Discovery Journey Rebellion Sacrifice	Your question should be a seminar style or *open-ended* question.	Videos Models/displays Artwork Original music Website/blog Animation	Literary examples Historical events Current events + Individual metacognition

Interdisciplinary Gallery Project Checklist

Requirements   **Due Date**

1. Form a *group* consisting of three to five people. _____

2. Select a *big idea* together. _____

3. Identify the *big question* together. _____

4. Obtain *approval* for your group's big question. _____

5. *Answer* the question using well-analyzed evidence from:
    - literary events (at least *two examples* from *two different* class texts)
    - a historical event
    - a current event. _____

6. Choose a *presentation format.*
    Come up with the clearest, deepest, most awesome format to answer the big question. _____

7. Make a *list of materials* needed for the gallery presentation. _____

8. Complete an individual metacognitive processing sheet.* _____

Metacognitive processing sheet requires the following elements:
   - Description of *your specific contribution* to the project.
   - Explanation of *what you have learned* from this project.

Created by Jessica Antonucci.

- annotated student drawings or photographs that connect to the course content
- graphic illustrations of course content (charts, graphs, concept maps, webs, time lines).

If you are a content area teacher, you will have to modify this list of possible items to include more accurate representations of work in your discipline-specific portfolio.

Teacher-2-Teacher

Our district formed a curriculum writing committee a few years ago for the English department. In addition to aligning the English language arts curriculum to the new standards, we began creating thematic units incorporating literature around an anchor text (including poetry, fiction, and nonfiction), content vocabulary, academic vocabulary, grammar, usage, and mechanics. Each unit generally runs a complete quarter (eighth grade has an additional unit) and now contains common assessments. Additionally, we created a portfolio assessment system. We developed one common prompt per quarter that must be included in the end-of-year portfolio. Even though the portfolio minimum requirements are identical for all Sachem Middle School students, teachers may opt to include additional pieces. Every portfolio must include the reflection piece and one revision. (See Figure 5.3 for the sixth-, seventh-, and eighth-grade end-of-year reflection task and Figure 5.4 for excerpts from an eighth grader's final reflection.)

Heather Stumpf, middle school English teacher and department chair

ROUTINE 2   Routines for Reflection and Celebration of Learning

In addition to synthesizing learning in your course and reviewing and assessing course content in alternative ways, remember to engage your students in routines that invite them to reflect and celebrate their learning. Donald Schon (1983) suggested that a critical capacity to develop is the ability to reflect in action (while the learning is taking place) and on action (after the learning taken place). Translating his ideas into the secondary classroom, students regularly engage in reflective activities throughout the year by self-assessing their performance, writing in journals and leaning logs, and using rubrics and checklists (in action). In addition, students also need time at the end of the year to look back on their learning processes and accomplishments (on action). Here are some routines to help students consider and share what they have learned.

SELF-EXAMINATION ROUTINES

When students are given time for self-examination, they develop mindfulness and social-emotional skills that might not have been explicitly included in the course content (Barell 1995). They are invited to reflect on their growth and learning in your content area as well as in their capacity as individual thinkers.

Sixth-Grade Reflection

The Greatest Challenge

Your task: Choose the piece of writing you felt was most challenging for you to produce and answer the questions that follow.

Title of your piece: _____

Type of writing (narrative/argument/informative): _____

Explain why this piece of writing was such a challenge. Was it the type of writing that you struggled with? Was it a grammatical skill that gave you trouble? Was the reading that accompanied the writing difficult for you? _____

_____

If you could write this piece again, in what ways would you do things differently? _____

_____

Seventh-Grade Reflection

A Piece That Shows Growth

Your task: Choose a piece of writing that shows your growth or improvement as a writer and answer the questions that follow.

Title of your piece: _____

Type of writing (narrative/argument/informative): _____

Explain which element (grammar, voice, vocabulary, etc.) of this piece of writing is the strongest and why. _____

_____

Choose an element of this piece of writing that was once a weakness for you and explain how your writing reflects improvement in that area. _____

_____

Eighth-Grade Reflection

Writing for High School and Beyond

Your task: Answer each question about your portfolio as a whole.

How does your writing portfolio show that you are ready to enter the next step of your life after middle school? _____

_____

What did you learn about yourself when you compiled the information at the end of the portfolio? _____

_____

Figure 5.4 Excerpt from an Eighth-Grader's Portfolio Reflection

My writing portfolio shows that I am ready to enter the next step of life after middle school. Compared to my elementary school years, my writing skills always seemed to be lacking for me, as I could think of many wonderful thoughts in my head, but could not seem to find the right words when it came to portraying it through writing for somebody else to read. It's like my brain couldn't process what my idea was when it came to printing or typing it on paper. Now that I'm in eighth grade I find it so much easier to portray my message and get my main theme across to the reader's mind. The pieces in my portfolio show both my personality and writing skills in a positive manner. I believe that my portfolio shows that I am ready to go on to high school.

When compiling the information at the end of my portfolio, I learned that I have started to express my feeling on topics and themes through my writing. I used to read a story and once it was over just leave it there, but now when I read, I start forming all these questions, opinions, and judgments. One short story I related to was "Flowers for Algernon." Just like Charlie has a mental disability, a girl I'm close with named Marissa was diagnosed with ROHHAD disease. Yes, I know that Marissa's disease is a physical one, but they both can't do specific activities because of their disabilities. Relationships like the one I have with Marissa give me better insight on what the characters are actually going through.

The accomplishment that makes me most proud is the increase in my grades for English. School is very important to me, as I'd like to attend a good college and achieve an important job. Although my middle school grades do not go on my college transcript, it shows me that I'm capable of producing well written essays which will come in handy in high school. It just makes me proud to know I'm getting good grades because I want to and not because anyone else wants me to.

Self-Evaluation and Goal Setting

Although most of your students will be thinking of grades when you ask them to self-assess, a more comprehensive and effective practice is to invite them to evaluate their learning process as well as the outcomes of your course and set goals for future learning. Having students use a weekly self-evaluation checklist to establish good study habits ensures that students understand how study skills and their learning routines affect their learning outcomes. You might try to have students self-evaluate quarterly, or at the very least, reflect at the end of the year.

You can use the checklist in Figure 5.5 to guide you in the creation of your own student self-evaluation.

Figure 5.5 End-of-Year Self-Evaluation Checklist

This Past Year	Rarely/Never	Sometimes	Always/Often
❏ I came to class prepared.			
❏ I completed all assignments.			
❏ I met all deadlines.			
❏ I participated actively during class discussions.			
❏ I took good notes during class (writing questions, using color, adding sketches, enumerating, circling, underlining, and drawing boxes around important information).			
❏ Whenever I had an exam, I planned several study sessions to actively review the material.			
❏ I used active skills to study for tests (writing, drawing, reciting, visualizing, generating my own questions and responses).			
❏ I told myself, "I can do this even though I haven't figured it out yet."			

After they complete a self-evaluation checklist, ask your students to reflect on what habits they might change to improve their learning next year. Use the following open stems for student response:

- **Something new that worked well for me this year was** _____
- **I feel good about** _____
- **I need to put more effort into** _____
- **To do even better next year, my goal is to** _____

Ask students to share out in small or large groups so they can hear what their peers have to say and learn from one another.

A different type of self-evaluation was reported by Sarah D. Sparks (2014) stating that a California High School (Da Vinci)

> regularly encourages students to examine their academic and emotional growth. At
> the end of each semester and before they graduate, students must give a talk before
> a panel of teachers on what they have learned in at least three classes, citing specific
> examples of mistakes made and problems overcome. (19)

Additionally, you can design an end-of-year self-assessment tool (checklist, rubric, rating scale, or open-ended questions) that is closely aligned to your course objectives and content standards.

CREATIVE EXPRESSIONS

Kieran Egan (2005) claims that "engaging students' imaginations is crucial to successful learning" (xi). He further notes that imagination is closely tied to students' emotional lives and advocates for the kind of education that involves their hopes, fears, and passion. Creative expressions as end-of-course routines will accomplish just that: Students may engage in creative writing such as producing poems, short stories, booklets for peers or younger grades, or memoirs or produce multimedia projects such as video clips and iMovies that they design, film, and star in. A final celebration of learning may be limited to a class "party" or may be expanded beyond the classroom walls and involve the entire school community.

COACH'S NOTES

My students create reflective e-portfolio presentations using a multimedia tool, like Prezi, to reflect on their learning journeys. Students include screenshots, links, and samples of their work for each unit or module. As they walk us through the presentation, they also share what they learned in each unit and how they will apply this knowledge to help them achieve their goals. These reflective portfolio presentations are published for their peers and families to view. Additionally, students create one collaborative advice presentation they pass on to the students who will take the course next year. Each student is responsible for sharing an organizational, time-saving, or studying tip. VoiceThread is a fantastic multimedia tool that allows for a collaborative presentation.

Shelly Sanchez Terrell, adjunct professor and teacher trainer

Memoir Writing

Dawn Latta Kirby and Dan Kirby (2007, 2010) introduced the Contemporary Memoir as a genre that may engage and energize student writers in secondary classrooms. Through memoir writing "students . . . come to some understanding of why they remember specific events, people, and places, and what those remembrances tell them about who they are now" (11). Students are asked to take more risks and assume more authorial responsibility for their final products since they are working on something very personal and unique. See how Michelle Ackerman's scaffolded outline positions students to achieve these goals as they write their end-of-year memoirs in a ninth-grade English class (Figure 5.6).

Figure 5.6 Directions to Write an End-of-Year Memoir in a Ninth-Grade English Class

Many of the best works of literature have a personal quality to them, and a personal connection to the life of their authors. Your assignment is to create your own memoir in the form of a personal newspaper. This will be a memoir of your childhood and your life today. You will be writing about the people, places, and events that have helped to shape you into the person you are today.

****

1. ***The Cover***: It must include your name and a catchy title. Decorate it as you wish.

2. ***The Table of Contents***: Your newspaper must have a table of contents. In the table of contents, you will list each section of your paper and the page where it can be found.

3. ***Me Back When***: This section should include stories and recollections from your past. Focus on birth, preschool days, early childhood, elementary school. (Tell stories about your past—what is your earliest memory?)

4. ***My Accomplishments***: Describe a project that you completed at some point in your life, along with an explanation of how you became interested in it. This accomplishment should be important to you.

5. ***People I Admire***: Tell who your role models are and why.

6. ***My Family and Me***: Describe your family members and what you think is special about each one.

7. ***My Biographer and Me***: This will be a one- or two-page biography of you, written by someone who knows you very well (a close friend, sibling, parent, or relative).

8. ***The Changing Me***: Discuss things about your life and yourself that you think are changing or that you would like to change if you could.

9. ***The Future Me/My Goals***: Discuss your short-term and long-term goals (plans) for the future (family, school, career). Talk about leisure activities, travel plans. Describe some of the things that you would like to do or learn in the near and distant future.

10. ***Movie Review***: Write a review of a movie that had a great impact upon you. Explain why it was so meaningful.

11. ***Television Show Review***: Write a review of your favorite TV show. Why does this show appeal to you?

12. ***Book Review/Music Review***: Write a review of a book or song that speaks to you. Share why it has such meaning for you.

Adapted with permission from Michelle Ackerman.

Letter to Freshmen

In the twenty-first century, teens (and their teachers) are much more likely to take out their cell phones to text each other and share photos on Instagram, send emails, or direct-message one another on Facebook or Twitter. Letter writing may become a dying art and form of self-expression and communication. We recommend infusing opportunities for writing letters (to self or others). See the following Teacher-2-Teacher to learn how Jeff Jakob uses letters to freshmen as an end-of-year routine that not only invites his class to write a letter to incoming students but also contributes to community building in his school. Figure 5.7 contains excerpts from two student letters written at the end of the year to welcome the incoming freshmen the following year.

Teacher-2-Teacher

Teaching freshmen, I recognize that there are a lot of misconceptions about high school and students tend to be nervous at the start of the year. A routine I use each year is to have my students reflect at the end of the year and write a letter to the incoming freshmen. Students share their favorite parts of class/high school, tips for success, advice, words of encouragement, and even examples of what not to do. The new students enjoy reading the letters, feel a sense of comfort after reading a few, have a preview of what the course/high school will be like, and look forward to writing their own letter at the end of the year. Handwritten letters work, but blogs are perfect for this activity!

Jeff M. Jakob, National Board–certified teacher

Figure 5.7 Excerpts from Letters to Freshmen

Letter to Freshmen

Your first day may or may not go so well. I know mine wasn't at all how I planned. I woke up late, missed my ride, and I even almost forgot my ID and backpack. The main thing to do on your first day is just take a deep breath and relax. Also, pay attention to the teachers and actually follow the rules.

Doing your work and staying out of trouble is easy to do. Just don't get mixed in the wrong crowd of people and you will be out of high school in no time.

I know one thing that helped me get through my freshman year was music. Music is a good thing to use when you need to study or even to just listen to. I'm not saying to just listen to it all the time, I'm saying you should find something that could help you stay on task with your work and motivation.

Yours Truly,

Chris G.

Dear Incoming Freshman,

Welcome to high school! Are you scared yet? Don't be, you will be fine, trust me. I felt the same exact way you did. High school is a lot of fun, but freshman year is a huge adjustment, and it's a rough one . . . the best advice I can give you is to be yourself, and make sure you do your work. If you are yourself, freshman year will be A LOT easier for you. Don't change to make someone else happy, or like you. It's not worth it, if they don't like you for who you are, then they aren't worth your time. I know it sounds harsh, but it's very true. There are about 3,000 students in the school, and billions of people in this world. There is a person for everyone, but don't change for just one person. Next, your school work, don't tune me out here, please! All of your teachers are going to be hounding you to do your work, and it's going to be annoying the first week, but they know what they are talking about . . . It's a lot, I'm not going to lie, but it is what you put in to it. If every day you wake up saying today is going to be horrible, well more than likely it will be, but if you walk in to those doors with a good happy positive attitude, then your day is going to start off well.

Good luck, and enjoy it!

Rachel R.

Video

An alternative to creative writing is using multimedia as a reflection tool. Creating a video clip on Movie Maker or making an iMovie is no longer out of reach for most schools. Students enjoy viewing themselves on movies that highlight their learning experiences. Although some teachers take pictures in their classes regularly and film their students throughout the year, another option is to have students become historians for the course and document key events through film and photography.

Teacher-2-Teacher

It is important to give students opportunities to celebrate and reflect on their learning. I try to design creative end-of-unit assessments that emphasize collaboration and performance. I frequently film my students' performances and play them back in class. Watching their performances allows my students to assess themselves and celebrate their achievements.

At the end of the year, I compile the footage into a highlights reel. The students' ten months of academic and socioemotional growth is evident when summarized in the ten-minute video. My students are proud to witness their development unfold before their eyes. Showing a highlight reel at the end of the year also gives students an opportunity to reflect on the year's essential questions and provides me feedback on how to improve future units and projects.

The only tools that I use to create these videos are the camera on my phone and the preinstalled video editor on my laptop. If you are unsure how to utilize the tools on your computer, I recommend watching instructional videos on YouTube.

Alex Corbitt, seventh-grade English teacher

End-of-Year Celebration

Many adolescents feel overwhelmed or exhausted by the end of the school year, or even at the end of shorter courses. You may be more than eager to wrap up the year as well. Nonetheless, your students need to recognize that progress has been made and it is time to celebrate.

Teacher-2-Teacher

I have learned that the most effective way to improve my students' reading and writing skills is by getting them to become vested in the writing process. If they are writing about something they are interested in, the process becomes a lot less daunting. My students write a ten-chapter autobiography over the course of the school year, which they present to their parents and the entire school community at our end-of-year Book Celebration Party.

The date is booked a year in advance. The invitations are made by students sent to family members and all teachers of past and present. Over 250 people arrive to view their scrapbook autobiography books adorned in all colors of the rainbow and every sticker available. Each book is unique with pictures, drawings, and memorabilia. They are placed on brightly decorated tables and displayed while the students proudly stand by their piece of art! Music resonates throughout the crowd and the aroma of international food delights are served by the proud parents of these celebrity students. This is a celebration of life, their LIFE in print (see Figures 5.8, 5.9, and 5.10).

Maryclaire Dumas, literacy specialist and teacher of English to speakers of other languages

Figure 5.8 Invitation to Attend the End-of-Year Celebration

Figures 5.9 and 5.10 Members of the School Community Enjoying the Student Display

Special Considerations

Your students (and their teachers, too) are getting ready for the summer vacation; many are moving from middle school to high school or from high school to post-secondary studies or vocational education. Ending the school year on a high note remains a priority. The challenges you have faced all year long regarding class size, schedules, and logistics will need to be addressed yet one more time.

What if you teach over 100 students each day?

You might be responsible for a large number of students, yet all the review routines we shared in this chapter are structured for small-group engagement. The group size will depend on your class size and the type of review that you are implementing. Individual projects that require closer monitoring may include peer review and small-group support rather than one-on-one teacher conferencing time.

What if you teach multiple courses each semester?

Because most of the end-of-course routines are highly student-centered and rely heavily on student-directed activities, even if you teach multiple courses, the routines for review and celebration will follow a similar format and engage students in collaborative tasks. "They persist longer, demonstrate higher self-efficacy, and formulate improved problem-solving skills during a challenging task when they see their peers doing the same" (Germeroth and Day-Hess 2013, 20).

What if you don't have your own classroom?

Traveling from classroom to classroom will present its own challenges at the end of the course just as much as it did throughout the year. Using technology tools may aid in accessing the materials you will need.

What if your class period is longer than the typical forty- to forty-four-minute class?

Class sessions that are sixty to ninety minutes long support the development and implementation of review and assessment practices. Additional time will be available to plan, create, and share projects; to review and self-assess course learning; and to reflect and celebrate as a community of learners.

What if you want to incorporate technology?

Many Apps and Web-based tools will readily support your learning goals for end-of-year routines. The jigsaw review can be done electronically so that students work collaboratively on a website you design or in the same Google Doc you set up. Many of the review projects we suggest can be presented using Web 2.0 technology. Rather than using class time for review presentations, student products can be uploaded so that all students can review and assess them at home or in a computer lab. At www.edu.glogster.com, students can create content online for products that include text, graphics, images, audio and video clips, and Web links. Visit Starr Sackstein's blog; She asks her students at the end of the year to create a brief video clip or Vox to reflect on what they have learned. She shares sample reflections on her blog at http://starrsackstein.com/category/students-learn-year/.

A Final Thought

Reflection, mindfulness, and celebration of achievement should be an integral part of learning in secondary classes. In a test-driven era, it takes courage and commitment as well as careful planning to designate time for nurturing life skills such as becoming self-regulated learners and reflective thinkers. When your students see that opportunities for these types of engagements are routinely offered, they internalize the need to pause and review, to stop and process, to self-assess, to set new goals, and to celebrate. It is our hope that as a result, they develop as increasingly more thoughtful, more self-directed, and more productive young adults.

Essential Questions for Individual Reflection, Collegial Circles, and Group Discussions

- *What is the central idea running through this chapter and how does it inform your instruction?*

- *Why is it important to create an opportunity for reflection and self-assessment in each course?*

- *How will you fit the recommended routines into the few available days at the end of your course?*

- *What challenges do you anticipate as you implement the suggested routines at the end of your course?*

- *How can you inspire your students to set achievable goals for the future?*

References

Alber, R. 2015. "Tools for Teaching: Managing a Large Class Size." Edutopia blog post. http://www
.edutopia.org/blog/managing-large-class-size-rebecca-alber.

Alderman, M. K. 2013. *Motivation for Achievement: Possibilities for Teaching and Learning.* Mahwah, NJ:
Lawrence Erlbaum Associates.

Allington, R. L. L., and R. E. Gabriel. 2012. "Every Child, Every Day." *Educational Leadership* 69 (6):
10–15.

Bandura, A. 1989. "Human Agency in Social Cognitive Theory." *American Psychologist* 44 (9):
1175–84.

_____. 1991. "Social Cognitive Theory of Self-Regulation." *Organizational Behavior and Human
Decision Processes* 50 (2): 248–87.

Barber, B. R. 1992. *An Aristocracy of Everyone: The Politics of Education and the Future of America.* New
York: Oxford University Press.

Barell, J. 1995. *Teaching for Thoughtfulness: Classroom Strategies to Enhance Intellectual Development.* 2d
ed. White Plains, NY: Longman.

Bear, D. R., M. Invernizzi, S. Templeton, and F. Johnston. 2012. *Words Their Way: Word Study for
Phonics, Vocabulary, and Spelling Instruction.* 5th ed. Upper Saddle River, NJ: Pearson.

Beck, I. L., M. G. McKeown, and L. Kucan. 2013. *Bringing Words to Life: Robust Vocabulary
Instruction.* 2d ed. New York: Guilford.

Beers, K., and R. E. Probst. 2012. *Notice and Note: Strategies for Close Reading.* Portsmouth, NH:
Heinemann.

Berger, W. 2014. *A More Beautiful Question: The Power of Inquiry to Spark Breakthrough Ideas.* New
York: Bloomsbury Publishing.

Blackburn, B. 2014. "Use Writing Activities to Bond with New Students." www.middleweb
.com/17277/use-writing-to-bond-with-students/.

Bloom, B. S. 1976. *Human Characteristics and School Learning.* New York: McGraw-Hill.

Bloom, S. J. and J. M. Smith. 1999. "Multicultural 'Autobio' Poem." *Electronic Magazine of
Multicultural Education.* www.eastern.edu/publications/emme/1999spring/bloom.html.

Boutz, A. L., H. F. Silver, and J. W. Jackson. 2013. *Tools for Thoughtful Assessment: Classroom-Ready
Techniques for Improving Teaching and Learning.* Franklin Lanes, NJ: Thoughtful Education Press.

Boyd, M. P., and S. Smyntek-Gworek. 2012. "Morning Meetings in a Third Grade Classroom:
Literacy and Learning." *Journal of Classroom Interaction* 47 (2): 4–12.

Bransford, J. D., A. L. Brown, and R. R. Cocking. 2004. *How People Learn.* Washington, DC:
National Academy Press.

Britton, J. N. 1970. *Language and Learning.* Miami: University of Miami Press.

Brookhart, S. M. 2014. *How to Design Questions and Tasks to Assess Student Thinking.* Alexandria, VA:
ASCD.

Buehl, D. 2001. *Classroom Strategies for Interactive Learning; Second Edition*. Newark, DE: International Reading Association.

———. 2009. *Classroom Strategies for Interactive Learning*. 3d ed. Newark DE: International Reading Association.

Burgess, D. 2012. *Teach Like a Pirate: Increase Student Engagement, Boost Your Creativity, and Transform Your Life as an Educator*. San Diego, CA: Dave Burgess Consulting.

Burke, J. 2012. *The English Teacher's Companion: A Completely New Guide to Classroom, Curriculum, and Profession*. 4th ed. Portsmouth, NH: Heinemann.

Burkins, J., and K. Yaris. 2013. "Top Ten Themes of IRA Convention 2013." Burkins and Yaris: Think Tank for 21st Century Literacy blog. April 23. www.burkinsandyaris.com/top-ten-themes -of-ira-convention-2013/.

Burris, C., and A. Aja. 2014. "The Myth of 'Equity' and Common Core." March 16. http:// dianeravitch.net/2014/03/16/burris-and-aja-the-myth-of-equity-and-common-core/.

Carpenter, S. 2012. "Testing Enhances the Transfer of Learning." *Current Directions in Psychological Science* 21 (5): 279–83. DOI: 10.1177/0963721412452728.

Caruso, J. 1999. "My Life in a Bag." *Electronic Magazine of Multicultural Education* 1 (4). www.eastern .edu/publications/emme/1999fall/caruso.html.

Cazden, C. B. 2001. *Classroom Discourse: The Language of Teaching and Learning*. 2d ed. Portsmouth, NH: Heinemann.

Collins, S. 2010. *The Hunger Games*. New York: Scholastic.

Costa, A. L. 1984. "A Reaction to Hunter's 'Knowing Teaching and Supervising.'" In *Using What We Know About Teaching*, edited by P. L. Hosford, 196–203. Alexandria, VA: Association for Supervision and Curriculum Development.

Costa, A. L., and B. Kallick. 2000. *Habits of Mind: A Developmental Series*. Alexandria, VA: ASCD.

Costigan, A. T. 2008. *Teaching Authentic Language Arts in a Test-Driven Era*. New York: Routledge.

Coxhead, A. 2000. "A New Academic Word List." *TESOL Quarterly* 34 (2): 213–38.

Cronsberry, J. 2004. "Word Walls: A Support for Literacy in the Secondary School Classroom." http://curriculum.org/storage/258/1334340769/World_Walls_-_A_Support_for_Literacy_in_ Secondary_School_Classrooms.pdf.

Dalton, B. W. 2010. "Motivation." In *Noncognitive Skills in the Classroom: New Perspectives on Educational Research*, edited by J. A. Rosen, E. J.. Glennie, B. W. Dalton, J. M. Lennon, and R. N. Bozick, 11–38. RTI Press publication No. BK-0004-1009. Research Triangle Park, NC: RTI International. http://rti.org/pubs/rtipress/rosen/chapter2_motivation.pdf. DOI:10.3768/ rtipress.2010.bk.0000.1009.

Danielson, C. 2013. "The Framework." www.danielsongroup.org/userfiles/files/downloads /2013EvaluationInstrument.pdf.

Davis, V. 2014. "Social Entrepreneurship: 7 Ways to Empower Student Changemakers." www.edutopia.org/blog/empowering-student-changemakers-vicki-davis.

Dean, C. B., E. R. Hubbell, H. Pitler, and B. Stone. 2012. *Classroom Instruction That Works: Research -Based Strategies for Increasing Student Achievement*. 2d ed. Alexandria, VA: ASCD.

Dewey, J. 1933. *How We Think: A Restatement of the Relation of Reflecting Teaching to the Educative Process*. Boston: D.C. Heath and Company.

Dodge, J. 2006. *Differentiation in Action*. New York: Scholastic.

———. 2009. *25 Quick Formative Assessments for a Differentiated Classroom*. New York: Scholastic.

Dodge, J., and A. Honigsfeld. 2014. *Core Instructional Routines: Go-To Structures for Literacy Learning in the K–5 Classroom*. Portsmouth, NH: Heinemann.

Duffelmeyer, F. 1994. "Effective Anticipation Guide Statements for Learning from Expository Prose." *Journal of Reading* 37: 452–55.

Education Week Research Center. 2014. "Engaging Students for Success: Findings from a National Survey." www.edweek.org/media/ewrc_engagingstudents_2014.pdf.

Egan, K. 2005. *An Imaginative Approach to Teaching*. San Francisco, CA: Jossey-Bass.

Ellroy, J. 2010. "The Last Spin." In *The Best American Noir of the Century*, 171–179. Boston: Houghton Mifflin Harcourt.

Esquith, R. 2007. *Teach Like Your Hair Is on Fire: Methods and Madness Inside Room 56*. New York: Penguin Books.

Faircloth, B. S. 2009. "Making the Most of Adolescence: Harnessing the Search for Identity to Understand Classroom Belonging." *Journal of Adolescent Research* 24: 321–48.

Fang, Z. 2012. "Approaches to Developing Content Area Literacies: A Synthesis and a Critique." *Journal of Adolescent & Adult Literacy* 56: 103–107. DOI:10.1002/JAAL.00110.

Farber, K. 2011. *Change the World with Service Learning: How to Organize, Lead, and Assess Service -Learning Projects*. Lanham, MD: Rowman and Littlefield.

Fisher, D., and N. Frey. n.d. *Background Knowledge: The Overlooked Factor in Reading Comprehension*. New York: McGraw Hill Education.

———. 2008. *Better Learning Through Structured Teaching: A Framework for the Gradual Release of Responsibility*. Alexandria, VA: ASCD.

———. 2009. *Background Knowledge: The Missing Piece of the Comprehension Puzzle*. Portsmouth, NH: Heinemann.

———. 2014a. *Better Learning Through Structured Teaching: A Framework for the Gradual Release of Responsibility*. 2d ed. Alexandria, VA: ASCD.

———. 2014b. "Speaking Volumes." *Educational Leadership* 72 (3): 18–23.

Fisher, D., N. Frey, and C. L. Uline. 2013. *Common Core English Language Arts in a PLC at Work, Leader's Guide*. Bloomington, IN: Solution Tree Press.

Fitch, K. G. 2013. "Routines and Producers to Start the Year Off Right." www.wholechildeducation. org/blog/routines-and-procedures-to-start-the-year-right.

Fusco, E. 2012. *Effective Questioning Strategies in the Classroom: A Step-by-Step Approach to Engaged Thinking and Learning, K–8*. New York: Teachers College Press.

Gallagher, K. 2009. *Readicide: How Schools Are Killing Reading and What You Can Do About It*. Portland, ME: Stenhouse.

———. 2011. *Write Like This: Teaching Real World Writing Through Modeling & Mentor Texts*. Portland, ME: Stenhouse.

Gallo, D. 1988. "On the Bridge." In *Visions: 19 Short Stories by Outstanding Writers for Young Adults*, 122–128. New York: Laurel Leaf Books.

Gee, J. P. 2003. *What Video Games Have to Teach Us About Learning and Literacy*. New York: Palgrave Macmillan.

Germeroth, C. and C. Day-Hess. 2013. *Self-Regulated Learning for Academic Success: How Do I Help Students Manage Their Thoughts, Behaviors, and Emotions?* Alexandria VA: ASCD.

Giouroukakis, V., and M. Connolly. 2012. *Getting to the Core of English Language Arts, Grades 6–12: How to Meet the Common Core State Standards with Lessons from the Classroom*. Thousand Oaks, CA: Corwin Press.

Glynn, C. 2001. *Learning on Their Feet: A Sourcebook for Kinesthetic Learning Across the Curriculum K–8*. Shoreham, VT: Discover Writing Press.

Goldenberg, C. N. 1992. *Instructional Conversations and Their Classroom Application*. Educational Practice Report 2. Santa Cruz: The National Center for Research on Cultural Diversity and Second Language Learning, University of California, Santa Cruz.

Gottlieb, M. 2011, November. *From Academic Language to Academic Success*. Workshop presented at the Iowa Culture & Language Conference, Coralville, IA.

Greene, J. P., B. Kisida, and D. H. Bowen. 2014. "The Value of Field Trips." *Education Next* 14 (1): 78–86.

Greene, J. P., C. Hitt, A. Kraybill, and C. A. Bogulski. 2015. "Learning from Live Theater: Students Realize Gains in Knowledge, Tolerance, and More." *Education Next* 15 (1): 54–61.

Hakuta, K., J. Zwiers, and S. Rutherford-Quach. 2013. *Stanford University Constructive Conversations* MOOC.

Hannaford, C. 2005. *Smart Moves: Why Learning Is Not All in Your Head*. 2d ed. Salt Lake City, UT: Great Rivers Books.

Harvey, B. 2014. "Social Studies: 'Who Needs It?' Everyone!" www.teachingquality.org/content/blogs /brison-harvey/social-studies-who-needs-it-everyone.

Harvey, S., and A. Goudvis. 2013. "Comprehension at the Core." *The Reading Teacher* 66 (6): 432–39.

Haskins, J. 1998. *Black, Blue and Gray: African Americans in the Civil War*. New York: Simon & Schuster.

Hattie, J. 2009. *Visible Learning*. New York: Routledge.

———. 2012. *Visible Learning for Teachers: Maximizing Impact on Learning*. London: Routledge.

Heath, C., and D. Heath. 2007. *Made to Stick: Why Some Ideas Survive and Others Die*. New York: Random House.

Honigsfeld, A., and M. G. Dove. 2013. *Common Core for the Not-So-Common Learner, Grades 6–12: English Language Arts Strategies*. Thousand Oaks, CA: Corwin.

Huang, W. H.-Y., and D. Soman. 2013. "A Practitioner's Guide to Gamification of Education." http://inside.rotman.utoronto.ca/behaviouraleconomicsinaction/files/2013/09/GuideGamification EducationDec2013.pdf.

Hunter, M. 1984. "Knowing, Teaching, and Supervising." In *Using What We Know About Teaching*, edited by P. L. Hosford, 169–92. Alexandria, VA: Association for Supervision and Curriculum Development.

Jackson, Y. 2011. *The Pedagogy of Confidence: Inspiring High Intellectual Performance in Urban Schools*. New York: Teachers College Press.

Jensen, E. 2005. *Teaching with the Brain in Mind*. Alexandria, VA: ASCD.

Kagan, S., and M. Kagan. 2009. *Kagan Cooperative Learning*. San Clemente, CA: Kagan Publishing.

Karp, S. 2013/2014. "The Problems with the Common Core." www.rethinkingschools.org/archive /28_02/28_02_karp.shtml.

Kinsella, K. 2012. "Cutting to the Core: Communicating on the Same Wavelength." *Language Magazine* 12 (4): 18–25.

Kintsch, W., and K. A. Rawson. 2005. "Comprehension." In *The Science of Reading: A Handbook*, edited by M. J. Snowling and C. Hulme, 209–226. Malden, MA: Blackwell.

Kirby, D. L., and D. Crovits. 2013. *Inside Out: Strategies for Teaching Writing*. Portsmouth, NH: Heinemann.

Kirby, D. L., and D. Kirby. 2007. *New Directions in Teaching Memoir: A Studio Workshop Approach*. Portsmouth, NH: Heinemann.

———. 2010. "Contemporary Memoir: A 21st Century Genre Ideal for Teens." *English Journal* 99 (4): 22–29.

Kittle, P. 2013. *Book Love: Developing Depth, Stamina, and Passion in Adolescent Readers*. Portsmouth, NH: Heinemann.

Lehmann, C. 2012. "What Good Are Standards, If Funding Varies?" www.nytimes.com /roomfordebate/2012/12/10/the-american-way-oflearning/teaching-standards-are-moot-when -funding-is-so-disparate.

Lemov, D. 2010. *Teach Like a Champion: 49 Techniques That Put Students on the Path to College*. San Francisco: Jossey-Bass.

Levine, L. N., L. Lukens, and B. A. Smallwood. 2013. "The GO TO Strategies: Scaffolding Options for Teachers of Language Learners, K–12." www.cal.org/content/download/1906/22045/file/go-to -strategies.pdf.

Lombardi, M. M. 2007. "Authentic Learning for the 21st Century: An Overview." https://net .educause.edu/ir/library/pdf/ELI3009.pdf.

Markham, T. 2012. *Project Based Learning: Design and Coaching Guide—Expert Tools for Innovation and Inquiry for K–12 Educators*. San Rafael, CA: Heart IQ Press.

Marzano, R. J. 2003. *What Works in Schools: Translating Research into Action*. Alexandria, VA: ASCD.

———. 2004. *Building Background Knowledge for Academic Achievement: Research on What Works in Schools*. Alexandria, VA: ASCD.

Marzano, R. J., and D. Pickering. 2005. *Building Academic Vocabulary: Teacher's Manual*. Alexandria, VA: Association for Supervision and Curriculum Development.

Marzano, R. J., D. Pickering, and T. Heflebower. 2011. *The Highly Engaged Classroom*. Bloomington, IN: Marzano Research.

Marzano, R. J., and J. A. Simms. 2013. *Vocabulary for the Common Core*. Bloomington, IN: Marzano Research Laboratory.

Michaels, S., M. C. O'Connor, M. W. Hall, with L. B. Resnick. 2010. *Accountable Talk: Classroom Conversation That Works*. Version 3.1. Pittsburgh, PA: University of Pittsburgh.

Miller, D. 2009. *The Book Whisperer: Awakening the Inner Reader in Every Child*. San Francisco, CA: Jossey-Bass.

Mitra, S. 2010. "SOLE: How to Bring Self-Organized Learning Environment to Your Community." http://www.ted.com/prize/sole_toolkit.

Moje, E. B., M. Overby, N. Tysvaer, and K. Morris. 2008. "The Complex World of Adolescent Literacy: Myths, Motivations, and Mysteries." *Harvard Educational Review* 78 (1): 108–54.

Morris, T. 2002. *The Art of Achievement: Mastering the 7 C's of Success in Business and Life*. Kansas City, MO: Andrews McNeel Publishing.

Moss, C. M., and S. M. Brookhart. 2012. *Learning Targets: Helping Students Aim for Understanding in Today's Lesson*. Alexandria, VA: Association for Supervision and Curriculum Development.

Murphy, P. K., I. A. G. Wilkinson, A. O. Soter, M. N. Hennessey, and J. F. Alexander. 2009. "Examining the Effects of Classroom Discussion on Students' High-Level Comprehension of Text: A Meta-Analysis." *Journal of Educational Psychology* 101: 740–64.

Myers, S., and J. Lambert. 2000. *Diversity Icebreakers: A Trainer's Guide*. Fredonia, NY: HR Press.

National Governors Association (NGA) Center for Best Practices and Council of Chief State School Officers (CCSSO). 2010. *Common Core State Standards for English Language Arts and Literacy in History/Social Studies, Science, and Technical Subjects*. Washington, DC: NGA Center for Best Practices and CCSSO. http://corestandards.org/assets/CCSSI_ELA%20Standards.pdf.

Novak, K. 2014. *UDL Now!: A Teacher's Monday-Morning Guide to Implementing Common Core Standards Using Universal Design for Learning*. Wakefield, MA: CAST Professional Publishing.

Parsons, J., L. Taylor, and University of Alberta. 2012. *Student Engagement: What Do We Know and What Should We Do?* Edmonton, Canada: University of Alberta.

Pauk, W., and R. J. Q. Owens. 2011. *How to Study in College*. 10th ed. Boston, MA: Cengage Learning.

Pearson, P. D., and M. Gallagher. 1983. "The Instruction of Reading Comprehension." *Contemporary Educational Psychology* 8: 317–44.

Perfetti, C., and J. Stafura. 2014. *Word Knowledge in a Theory of Reading Comprehension*. Scientific Studies of Reading 18:22–37.

Piaget, J. 1952. *The Origins of Intelligence in Children*. M. Cook, trans. New York: International Universities Press.

Pink, D. 2009. *Drive: The Surprising Truth About What Motivates Us*. New York: Riverhead Books.

Popham, W. J. 2013. *Evaluating America's Teachers: Mission Possible?* Thousand Oaks, CA: Corwin.

Price-Mitchell, M. 2010. *Civic Learning at the Edge: Transformative Stories of Highly Engaged Youth*. Doctoral Dissertation, Fielding Graduate University.

Rao, A. 2012. "21st Century Icebreakers: 13 Ways To Get To Know Your Students with Technology." http://teachbytes.com/2012/08/05/21st-century-icebreakers-10-ways-to-get-to-know-your-students-with-technology/.

Ravitch, D. 2013. *Reign of Error: The Hoax of the Privatization Movement and the Danger to America's Public Schools.* New York: Alfred A. Knopf.

Remarque, E. M. 1987. *All Quiet on the Western Front.* New York: Ballantyne Books.

Richmond, E. 2014. "Study: Surprising Student Benefits to Live Theater Field Trips." December 8. www.ewa.org/blog-educated-reporter/study-surprising-student-benefits-live-theater-field-trips.

Ripp, P. 2014. *Passionate Learners: Giving Our Classroom Back to Our Students.* Virginia Beach, VA: Powerful Learning Press.

Ritchhart, R., M. Church, and K. Morrison. 2011. *Making Thinking Visible: How to Promote Engagement, Understanding, and Independence for All Learners.* San Francisco, CA: Jossey-Bass.

Rothstein, D., and L. Santana. 2011. *Make Just One Change: Teach Students to Ask Their Own Questions.* Cambridge, MA: Harvard Education Press.

Rothstein, D., and L. Santana. 2014. The right questions. *Educational Leadership* 72 (2). Online only. Retrieved from http://www.ascd.org/publications/educational-leadership/oct14/vol72/num02/The-Right-Questions.aspx on July 4, 2015.

Sanchez, N. M., and L. D. Harper. 2012. *Intentional Interaction: Research-Based Model for Content and Language Learning.* 2030 Press.

Scardamalia, M., and C. Bereiter. 1991. "Higher Levels of Agency for Children in Knowledge-Building: A Challenge for the Design of New Knowledge Media." *Journal of the Learning Sciences* 1 (1): 37–68.

Schon, D. 1983. *The Reflective Practitioner: How Professionals Think in Action.* London, UK: Temple Smith.

Schwartz, K. 2015. "How Inquiry Can Enable Students to Become Modern Day de Tocquevilles." http://blogs.kqed.org/mindshift/2015/02/how-inquiry-can-enable-students-to-become-modern-day-de-tocquevilles/.

Shanahan, T., and C. Shanahan. 2008. "Teaching Disciplinary Literacy to Adolescents: Rethinking Content-Area Literacy." *Harvard Educational Review* 78 (1): 40–59.

Shapiro, J. 2014. "Tapping into the Potential of Video Games and Uninhibited Play for Learning." http://blogs.kqed.org/mindshift/2014/04/tapping-into-the-potential-of-video-games-and-uninhibited-play-for-learning-education/.

Sheehy, K. 2013. "Student Engagement Nosedives in High School." www.usnews.com/education/blogs/high-school-notes/2013/01/16/student-engagement-nosedives-in-high-school.

Silver Strong and Associates. 2015. *Conversations with the Thoughtful Classroom* Webinar Series. http://www.thoughtfulclassroom.com/index.php?act=viewProd&productId=267.

Soper, T. 2015. "Free Field Trip: Google Is Paying Teachers to Have Students Watch Civil Rights Movie 'Selma'." February 13. www.geekwire.com/2015/free-field-trip-google-paying-teachers-students-watch-civil-rights-movie-selma/.

Sousa, D. A. 2008. *Mind, Brain, and Education: Neuroscience Implications for the Classroom.* Bloomington, IN: Solution Tree.

Sousa, D. A. 2011a. *How the Brain Learns.* 4th ed. Thousand Oaks, CA: Corwin Press.

Sousa, D. A. 2011b. *How the ELL Brain Learns.* Thousand Oaks, CA: Corwin Press.

Sparks, S. D. 2014. "California School Draws Lessons from Failure." *Education Week* 33 (34): 17–19.

Stern, M. 2012. *Evaluating and Promoting Positive School Attitude in Adolescents.* New York: Springer.

Stump, S. 2014. "Blast from the Past: Teacher Mails Letters Students Wrote Themselves 20 Years Ago." www.today.com/news/blast-past-teacher-mails-letters-students-wrote-themselves-20-years-2D79496258.

Stumpenhorst, J. 2013. *Innovation Day—The Trilogy.* http://stumpteacher.blogspot.com/2013/02/innovation-day-trilogy.html.

TCI. 1999. *History Alive! Interactive Student Notebook Manual.* Rancho Cordova, CA: Teacher's Curriculum Institute.

Tharp, R., and R. Gallimore. 1991. "The Instructional Conversation: Teaching and Learning in Social Activity." http://files.eric.ed.gov/fulltext/ED341254.pdf.

Tomlinson, C. A. 1999. *The Differentiated Classroom: Responding to the Needs of All Learners.* Alexandria, VA: ASCD.

_____. 2001. *How to Differentiate Instruction in Mixed-Ability Classrooms.* 2d ed. Alexandria, VA: ASCD.

Tomlinson, C. A., and C. A. Strickland. 2005. *Differentiation in Practice: A Resource Guide for Differentiating Curriculum, Grades 9–12.* Alexandria, VA: ASCD.

Tomlinson, C. A., and C. C. Eidson. 2003. *Differentiation in Practice: A Resource Guide for Differentiating Curriculum, Grades 5–9.* Alexandria, VA: ASCD.

Troia, G. A. 2007. "Research on Writing: Knowledge Development, Effective Interventions, and Assessment." *Reading and Writing Quarterly* 23 (3): 203–205.

Venn, J. J. 2007. *Assessing Students with Special Needs.* 4th ed. Upper Saddle River, NJ: Prentice Hall.

Vonnegut, K. 1968. "Harrison Bergeron." In *Welcome to the Monkey House: A Collection of Short Works.* New York: Delacorte Press.

Vygotsky, L. S. 1978. *Mind in Society: The Development of Higher Psychological Processes.* Cambridge, MA: Harvard University Press.

Washor, E., and C. Mojkowski. 2013. *Leaving to Learn: How Out-of-School Learning Increases Student Engagement and Reduces Dropout Rates.* Portsmouth, NH: Heinemann.

Wentzel, K. R., and A. Wigfield. 2009. "Introduction." In *Handbook of Motivation at School*, edited by K. R. Wentzel and A. Wigfield, 1–8. New York: Routledge.

Weissbourd, R., S. Jones, T. R. Anderson, J. Kahn, and M. Russell. 2014. *The Children We Mean to Raise: The Real Message Adults Are Sending About Values. Executive Summary.* http://sites.gse.harvard.edu/sites/default/files/making-caring-common/files/mcc_report_the_children_we_mean_to_raise_0.pdf

Wiesel, E. 2006. *Night*. New York: Hill and Wang.

Wiggins, G., and J. McTighe. 1998. *Understanding by Design*. Alexandria, VA: ASCD.

_____. 2005. *Understanding by Design*. 2d ed. Alexandria, VA: ASCD.

Williamson, R., and B. R. Blackburn. 2009a. "Beginnings and Endings: A Reflection of School Culture." *Instructional Leader* (July): 6–8.

_____. 2009b. A School Culture Audit. *Principal Leadership* (October): 60–62.

Wolsey, T. D., D. Lapp, and D. Fisher. 2010. "Breaking the Mold in Secondary Schools: Creating a Culture of Literacy." In *Breaking the Mold of School Instruction and Organization*, edited by A. Honigsfeld and A. Cohan, 9–16. New York: Rowman & Littlefield.

Wong, H. K., and R. W. Wong. 2004. *The First Days of School*. Mountain View, CA: Harry K. Wong Publications.

Wong Fillmore, L. 2012. *Supporting Access to the Language and Content of Complex Texts for EL and LM Students*. www.cgcs.org/cms/lib/DC00001581/Centricity/Domain/25/ELA_retreat-Wong%20 Fillmorepart2.pdf.

Wood, D., J. S. Bruner, and G. Ross. 1976. "The Role of Tutoring in Problem Solving." *Journal of Child Psychology and Psychiatry and Allied Disciplines* 17 (2): 89–100.

Wood, K. D., D. Lapp, J. Flood, and D. B. Taylor. 2008. *Guiding Readers Through Text: Strategy Guides for New Times*. 2d ed. Newark, DE: International Reading Association.

Wormeli, R. 2003. *Day One and Beyond: Practical Matters for New Middle-Level Teacher*. Stenhouse.

Yazzie-Mintz, E, and K. McCormick. 2012. "Finding the Humanity in the Data: Understanding, Measuring, and Strengthening Student Engagement." In *Handbook of Research on Student Engagement*, edited by S. L. Christenson et al., 743–61. New York: Springer.

Zike, D., and Glencoe Publishing Co. 2000. *Dinah Zike's Teaching with Foldables Mathematics: Dinah Zike's Teaching with Foldables Science*. New York: McGraw-Hill Glencoe.

Zwiers, J., and M. Crawford. 2011. *Academic Conversations: Classroom Talk That Fosters Critical Thinking and Content Understandings*. Portland, ME: Stenhouse.

Zwiers, J., S. O'Hara, and R. H. Pritchard. 2014. *Common Core Standards in Diverse Classrooms: Essential Practices for Developing Academic Language and Disciplinary Literacy*. Portland, MA: Stenhouse.

Index

A

Abel-Palmieri, Lisa M., 111
Academic conversations, 74–75
Academic journal routine, 53–55
Academic vocabulary routines, 37–41, 45, 71–78
Accountable talk routine, 74–75
Ackerman, Michelle, 136–137
Alderman, M. Kay, 3
All about me cinquain autobiographical poem, 7
Alphabet round-up routine, 85–87
Alternative assessment routines, 129–132
Anchor charts, 14, 45, 49, 72
Anchor projects routine, 107–108
Andrade, Mary, 68
Anticipation guide routine, 62–65
Antonucci, Jessica, 102, 104, 106, 130, 131
Application routines, 128–129
Artifact round up, 13
Artifact round up routine, 13
Association for Supervision and Curriculum
        Development (ASCD), 20
Association Triangles routine, 36–37
Autobiographical poems routine, 6–7

B

Background knowledge, building, 19, 61
Back-to-back protocol, 44
Backwards lesson design, 61
Baran, Brittany, 80
Basic literacy, 47
Bear, Donald, 41
Beck, Isabel, 37, 41
Beginning of year routines, icebreakers, 4–10
Beginning-of-class routines
blooming questions, 33–34
    focusing and guiding routines, 31–32
    learning targets, 32–33
    partners' inquiry, 34–36
Beginning-of-unit routines
    anticipation guide, 62–65
    virtual exploration, 65–66
Beginning-of-year routines

artifact round up, 13
autobiographical poems, 6–7
carousel brainstorming, 19
class rules and promises, 14–16
collaborative class, 14–16
collage, 10
contracts, course outlines, and letters to
        students, 16
course trailer or teaser, 17–18
for establishing a positive learning
        environment, 10–16
find someone who, 11
flexible grouping, 11–13
future self, 23–24
getting-to-know-you, 6–10
hopes and fears, 5
igniting passion for your course, 17–23
interest inventories, 8–9
nurturing habits of mind, 19–20
photo essay, 10
scavenger hunt in the textbook, 17
string conversation together, 6
time capsule, 23
vision letter, 23
visual tour, 17–18
yarn-to-yarn, 6
Berger, Michelle, 44
Berger, Warren, 59
Bing, Lisa, 13
Blackburn, Barbara, 3–4, 23, 127
Blackstone, Matt, 23
Blooming questions, 33–34
Bloom's taxonomy, 34
Book celebration party routine, 140
Boyd, Maureen, xi
Brainstorming routine, 19
Brandt, Hilcia, 32, 91
Brave Boys of Greensboro, The (play), 105
Britton, James, 85
Brookhart, Susan M., 50
Brown, Stephanie, 44
Burkins, Jan, x

C

Corio, Maureen, 43
Carousel brainstorming routine, 19
Carpenter, Shana, 128
Cazden, Courtney, 99
Celebrating and sharing reading routine, 105–107
Choice exit cards routine, 53
Choice homework night routine, 78–79
Church, Mark, xi
Class matrix, 15–16
Class rules and promises routine, 14–16
Classroom
    as a community of learners, xii
    culture, xi–xii, 3
    diversity in, 24
    gamified, 114–115
    special considerations in the, 24–25
    technology in the, 26
Close reading routine, 48
Code breakers, 47–48
Coffeehouse book chat, 104
Collaborative processing routine, 47
Collaborative routines
    class rules and promises, 14–16
    contracts, course outlines, and letters to
        students, 16
    for review, 85–92
Collage routine, photo, 10
Collegial circles, questions for, 58
Column note taking routine, 50
Common Core State Standards (CCSS), ix,
    32–33, 38, 115
Community engagement routines, 118–119
Community of learners, xii
Community-building routines
    artifact round up, 13
    find someone who., 10–11
    flexible grouping, 11–13
    "my life in a bag," 13
    people search, 10–11
Connolly, Maureen, 67
Constructive conservation skills poster, 76
Contemporary memoir, 136
Contract & Course outline routines, 16
Conversation Analysis Tool, 75

Conversations with the Thoughtful Classroom
    webinar, 36–37
Corbitt, Alex, 65, 139
Costa, Art, 19
Costigan, Arthur, 128
Course trailer or teaser, 17
Creative expressions routine, 140
Credibility, teacher, 3
Cronsberry, Jennifer, 41
Culture
    classroom, xi–xii
    for literacy, 99–100
    school, 3–4
Curriculum design process, 30

D

Daily lesson routines, 30–32
Dalton, Ben, 3
Danvers, Vaughan, 105
Davis, Vicki, ix
Dawn, Latta Kirby, 136
Dialectical journals routine, 52
Diaz, Michele, 72
Disciplinary literacy, 47
Diversity, 24
Double-entry journals routine, 52
Drop Everything and Read (DEAR), 101
Dumas, Maryclaire, 140
Dunbar, Paul Laurence, 105
D'Water, April, 112–113

E

Education Week Research Center, 3
Egan, Kieran, 136
End-of-class routines
    academic journals/learning logs, 53–55
    exit and choice exit cards, 53
End-of-course routines, 53
    alternative assessment, 129–132
    application, 128–129
    celebration routines, 140
    creative expressions, 136
    final projects, 129–130, 131
    jigsaw review, 127–128
    letter to freshman, 138–139
    memoir writing, 136–137

portfolios routine, 130, 132
reflection and celebration of learning, 132–140
review, 127–129
self-evaluation and goal setting, 134–135
self-examination, 132–134
student-generated assessments, 129
for synthesizing course learning, 127–129
video, 139
End-of-unit routines
alphabet round-up, 85–87
MathChat! 91–92, 93
stations, 88–90
text talk, 90–91
ThinkTank, 47, 87–88
End-of-Year celebration routines, 140
Esquith, Rafe, 97
Essential questions, 26, 56, 58, 96, 124, 142
Exhibition routine, 69–71
Exit cards routine, 53

F

Faircloth, Beverly, 6
Family learning experiences routines, 121
Farber, Katy, 118–119
Farrer, Bruce, 23
FedEx day, 112
Feldman, Brooke, 115–116
Field trip routine, 119–121
Fillmore, Lily Wong, 72–73
Final project routines, 129–130, 131
Find someone who. routine, 11
First impression routines
hopes and fears, 5
yarn-to-yarn, 6
Fisher, Douglas, xi, 29, 30, 41, 60, 61
Fitch, Kerry Grisworld, 4, 25
Flexible grouping routine
outer-circle tasks, 46
socratic circles, 45–47
ThinkTank, 47
Flexible grouping routines, defined, 42–44
Focus lesson routine, 61
Focusing and guiding routines, 31–32
Foldable routine, 80–84
Frey, Nancy, xi, 29, 30, 41, 60, 61
Future self routine, 23–24

G

Gallagher, Kelly, 100
Games for learning routine, 114–117
Gamification, 115
Garfinkel, Josh, 107
Gee, James, 114
Genius hour routines, 112–114
Getting-to-know-you routines
autobiographical poems, 6–8
collage, 10
interest inventories, 8–9
photo essay, 10
Getting-to-know-yourself as a learner routine,
21–22
Giosi, Ken, 109
Giouroukakis, Vicky, 67
Gnatt chart, 111
Goal-setting routines
getting to know yourself as a learner, 21–22
time capsule, 23
Grosskreutz, Edward, 121
Group discussions, questions for, 58
Group roles, 11–12
Group/individual presentations, 106–107
Grouping, flexible, 11–13, 23, 42–47
Guest speaker routine, 119–121
Guided instruction routine, 61
Gural, Michelle, 56

H

Habits of the Mind (Costa and Kallick), 19–20
Half Class/Half Class structure, 43
Harvey, Brison, xii
Hattie, John, xiii, 3, 20–21, 29, 30, 58, 125
High School Survey of Student Engagement
(HSSSE), ix
Homework routines, 78–84
Hopes and fears routine, 5
Hsiao, Lillian, 120–121
Hunter, Madeleine, 29, 61

I

"I am" autobiographical poem routine, 7
"I used to be, but now" autobiographical poem
routine, 7

Icebreakers
    first impression routines, 5–6
    getting-to-know-you routines, 6–10
Igniting passion for your course routines
    goal-setting, 20–21
    for previews, 17–18
    for review, 17
Independent reading routine
    getting started with, 101–102
    importance of, 99–101
Independent reading routines, celebrating and
        sharing reading, 105–107
Individual/group presentations, 106–107
Innovation day routines, 112–114
Instructional conversations, 75
Intentional Interaction Model, 75
Interactions with others routine, 103–104
Interactive notebooks routine, 50–51
Interdisciplinary Gallery, 131
Interest inventories, 8–9
Intermediate literacy, 47
International Reading Association Conference, x
International Reading Association
        ReadWriteThink website, 45
Inventories routine, 8–9
Irving, Barrington Captain, 123
Ito, Joichi, 59

J

Jakob, Jeff M., 57, 95–96, 138
Jigsaw review routine, 127–128

K

Kallick, Bena, 19
Kazantzakis, Nikos, 27
Kinsella, Kate, 75
Kirby, Dan, 136
Kittilsen, Vanessa, 110
Kittle, Penny, 103
Krajewski, Sarah, 100
Kucan, Linda, 37, 41

L

Layer, George, 56
Learning
    impact on, xiii

lesson plans and, 29
    objectives, 29
    phases of instruction for, 61
    student-driven, 98–99
Learning environment, establishing a positive, 10
Learning logs routine, 53–55
Learning targets, 3, 32–33
Lentino, Amanda, 101
Lesson design, 29–30, 31, 61
Lesson plans, designing, 29–30
Lesson summary and reflection routines
    academic journals/learning logs, 53–55
    exit and choice exit cards, 53
Letter to freshman routine, 138–139
Letters to students/families, 16
Lindquist, Robert, x
Line-by-line scaffolds for an autographical poem
        routine, 7–8
Literacy skills, 4–10, 47–48
Logan, Anne, 71
Lombardi, Marilyn M., 118
Long, Nicole A., 66
Lynch, Christian, 13
Lynn Darene Harper, 75

M

Making arguments routine, 67
Markham, Thom, 109
Marking period routines
    anchor projects, 107–108
    celebrating and sharing reading, 105–107
    family learning experience, 121
    field trip / guest speaker, 119–121
    games for learning, 114–117
    genius hour, 112–114
    independent reading, 99–107
    mini-research project, 108–109
    project-based learning, 109–111
    self-organized learning environment routine
        (SOLE), 114
    service-learning, 118–119
    student-directed learning, 107–117
    sustained independent reading, 102–104
    sustained silent reading (SSR), 101
Marzano, Robert, 19, 30, 71
MathChat! 91–92, 93

Mattes, Lee, 115
McDermott, Carrie, 15–16, 109
McKeown, Margaret, 37, 41
Meaning-making routines
    exhibition routine, 69–70
    making arguments, 67
Mechanic, Laurence, 109
Memoir routines, 136–137
Messman, Tyler, 112–113
Meyer, Kaitlin, 50
Middle-of-class routines
    academic vocabulary, 37–41, 71–78
    association triangles, 36–37
    close reading, 48
    column note taking, 50
    dialectical journals, 52
    interactive notebooks, 50–51
    lesson summary and reflection routines, 53–55
    note-taking, 48–49
    processing routines, 36–42
    reflect and connect, 36–37
    scaffolded notes, 49–50
    skill-building, 47–48
    socratic circles, 45–47
    stop-and-jot, 41–42
    ThinkTank, 47, 87–88
    turn-and-talk, 41–42
Middle-of-unit routines
    choice homework night, 78–79
    exhibition, 69–71
    foldable, 80–84
    making arguments, 67
    sentence level, 72–74
    S-O-S, 67–68
    Talk-About, 74–78
    text-level, 74
    word-level, 71–72
Mini-research projects, 108–109
Moje, Elizabeth Birr, 99
Morris, Karen, 99
Morris, Tom, 125
Morrison, Karin, xi
Motivation, student, 3, 24, 98–99, 100, 102, 105
Motivation theory, 3
"My Life in a Bag," 13

N
National Mole Day, 115
New Generation of Science Standards, 20
No Child Left Behind, ix
Note-taking routines
    column note taking, 50
    dialectical journals, 52
    how-to take notes, 48–49
    interactive notebooks, 50–51
    scaffolded notes, 49–50
Novak, Katie, 30

O
Outer-circle tasks, 46
Outside-the-classroom routines
    family learning experience, 121
    field trip / guest speaker, 119–121
    service-learning, 118–119
Overby, Melanie, 99

P
Partners' inquiry, 34–36
Pearsall, Christine, 71
People search, 11
Photo Essay routine, 10
Pink, Daniel, 112
Portfolios routine, 130, 132
Potter, Katie, 70–71
Powerful questioning routines, 33–34
Presentations, individual/group, 106–107
Processing routines
    academic vocabulary, 37–41, 71–78
    reflect and connect, 36–37
    stop-and-jot, 41–42
    turn-and-talk, 41–42
Project-based learning, 109–111
Projects through reading, 105–106
Public service announcement, 108

Q
QR codes, 26, 71–72
Question kiosk, 36
Questioning routines, powerful, 33–34

R
Rand, Michelle, 89–90

Rao, Aditi, 26

Readicide: How Schools Are Killing Reading and What you Can Do About It (Gallagher), 100

Reading, active, 47–48

Reading interest inventories, 8–9

Reading reflections, 103

Reflect and connect, 36–37

Reflection and celebration of learning, 132–140

Research

 and designing instructional units, 60–61

 and designing lessons, 29–30

 review, self-assessment and reflection, 126–127

 and student-driven learning experiences, 98–99

 and well-established routines, 3–4

Resources

 book discussion, 104

 formative assessment, 54

 getting-to-know-you routines, 10

 Habits of the Mind thinking, 20

 icebreakers, 10

 project-based learning, 112

 student motivation and engagement, 24

 vocabulary, 41

Review routines, 127–129

Ripp, Pernille, 14

Ritchhart, Ron, xi

Roder, Rich, 92

Routines

 academic language, 71–78

 beginning of class, 31–34

 for beginning-of-unit, 62–66

 for daily lessons, 30–31

 defined, xi

 end-of-unit, 85–92

 establishing, xv–xvi

 getting-to-know-you, 6–10

 goal-setting, 21–23

 homework, 74–84

 icebreakers, 5–10

 igniting passion for your course, 17–18, 20–21

 independent reading, 99–101

 middle-of-class routines, 53–55

 note-taking skills, 48–52

 outside of classroom, 118–121

 for previews, 17–18

 for reviews, 19–20

 self-evaluation and goal setting, 132–134

 See also Beginning of year routines; Beginning-of-class routines; Collaborative review routines; Community-building routines; Daily lesson routines; End-of-class routines; End-of-course routines; End-of-unit routines; First impression routines; Marking Period Routines; Middle-of-class routines; Middle-of-unit routines; Processing routines; Student-directed learning routines; Unit Routines

S

Sanchez, Nicole Marie, 75

Scaffolded notes, 49–50

Scavenger hunt in the textbook, 17

Schon, Donald, 132

Self-efficacy, 3

Self-evaluation and goal setting, 134–135

Self-evaluation questions, 55, 78

Self-examination routines, 132–134

Self-organized learning environment routine (SOLE), 114

Sentence cross-examination/dissection, 72–74

Sentence starters foldable, 76

Sentence-level routines, 72–74

Service-learning routine, 118–119

Shapiro, Jordan, 115

Sharing reading and celebrating routine, 105–107

Simms, Julia, 71

Skill-building routines, 47–48

Skype, 66

Smyntek-Gworek, Sylvia, xi

Socratic circles, 45–47

S-O-S routine, 67–69

Sousa, David, 31–32, 53, 77, 96

Sparks, Sarah D., 135

Special considerations, 24–25, 55–57, 92, 94–95, 121–123, 141–142

Stations routine, 88–90

Stop-and-jot, 41–42

Strickland, Cindy A., 43

String conversation together routine, 6

student, teacher relationships, 3

Student-directed learning routines

 anchor projects, 107–108

games for learning, 114–117
mini-research project, 108–109
project-based learning, 109–111
self-organized learning environment routine (SOLE), 114
Student-generated assessments routines, 129
Stumpenhorst, Josh, 112
Stumpf, Heather, 108, 132
Sustained independent reading, 102–104
Sustained silent reading (SSR), 101
SWRLing (speaking, writing, reading, and listening), x, 6, 38
Synthesizing course learning, 127–129

T

Talk-About routine, 74–78
Teacher, student relationships, 3
Teacher-learning cycle, 3
Technology tools, 66, 138–139
Terrell, Shelly Sanchez, 136
Text talk routine, 90–91
Text-level routine, 74
Thinking, levels of, 33–34
ThinkTank routine, 23, 47, 87–88
Three-Minute Pause, 55
Time capsule routine, 23
Tomlinson, Carol Ann, 43, 107–117
Turn-and-talk routine, 41–42
Tysvaer, Nicole, 99

U

Unit routines
academic language, 71–78
accountable talk routine, 74–75
alphabet round-up, 85–87
anticipation guide, 62–65
choice homework night, 78–79
collaborative review, 85–92
exhibition, 69–71
foldable, 80–84
homework routines, 78–84
making arguments, 67

MathChat! 87–88, 91–92, 93
sentence-level, 72–74
S-O-S, 67–69
stations, 88–90
talk-about, 74–78
text talk, 90–91
text-level, 74
ThinkTank, 23, 47
virtual exploration, 65–66
word-level, 71–72
Universal design for learning, 30

V

van Gogh, Vincent, 1
van Wie, Ellen, 119–120
Video routine, 139
Virtual exploration routine, 65–66
Visible Learning for Teacher (Hattie), xiii
Vision letter routine, 23
Visual tour routine, 17–18
Vocabulary, 37–41, 45, 71–78, 85–87

W

"We Wear the Mask" (Dunbar), 105
Wentzel, Kathryn R., 98
Whitaker, Todd, 27
Wigfield, Allan, 98
William, Melissa Nankin, 4
Williamson, Ronald, 3–4, 127
Woods, Ramona, 88
Word wall, interactive academic, 39
Word-level routine, 71–72
Words, tier 2 and tier 3, 38
Wormelli, Rick, 4

Y

Yaris, Kim, x
Yarn-to-yarn routine, 6

Z

Zehr, Mary Ann, 18
Zike, Dinah, 80

DATE DUE